ASSET ALLOCATION FOR INSTITUTIONAL PORTFOLIOS

ASSET ALLOCATION FOR INSTITUTIONAL PORTFOLIOS

Mark Kritzman, C.F.A.

BUSINESS ONE IRWIN
Homewood, Illinois 60430

For My Parents

This publication is designed to provide accurate and
authoritative information in regard to the subject matter
covered. It is sold with the understanding that neither the
author nor the publisher is engaged in rendering legal, accounting,
or other professional service. If legal advice or other expert
assistance is required, the services of a competent
professional person should be sought.

*From a Declaration of Principles jointly adopted by a Committee
of the American Bar Association and a Committee of Publishers.*

Project editor: Karen J. Murphy
Production manager: Ann Cassady
Jacket design: Michael S. Finkelman
Compositor: Ampersand Publisher Services, Inc.
Typeface: 11/13 Times Roman
Printer: Arcata Graphics/Kingsport

Library of Congress Cataloging-in-Publication Data

Kritzman, Mark P.
    Asset allocation for institutional portfolios / Mark Kritzman.
        p.   cm.
    ISBN 1-55623-163-6
    1. Institutional investments. 2. Portfolio management.
    I. Title.
    HG4521.K74 1990
    332.6—dc20   90–31612
                                                        CIP

Printed in the United States of America
1 2 3 4 5 6 7 8 9 0   K   7 6 5 4 3 2 1 0

PREFACE

Why do institutional investors typically allocate 60 percent of their fund to stocks and 40 percent to bonds? This book may not answer this question. It will, however, help you determine whether or not such an allocation is appropriate, and if not, what asset mix is most suitable for your fund.

Clearly, asset allocation is one of the most important decisions an investor will face, if not the most important decision. For example, imagine you had invested each month with perfect foresight in the asset class—stocks or bonds—with the higher return for that month for 10 years ending in 1987. You would have realized a return of 41 percent per year and, under this strategy, an initial $100 investment would have grown to $3,116 by the end of the period. Moreover, such accuracy would have added 28 percent annually to a passive alternative of investing $100 equally between stocks and bonds at the beginning of the period, resulting in more than a 30-fold increase in wealth.

The potential gain from asset allocation, not to mention the oppor tunity to control risk more effectively, certainly justifies the explosive growth in asset allocation activity. In addition to these motivations, though, interest in asset allocation has been facilitated by several institutional developments. Today, investors who choose to exercise discretion in asset allocation have at their disposal financial futures, index options, and program trading. Moreover, innovation in asset allocation technology has advanced rapidly in the past few years such that virtually any achievable risk preference can be produced mechanically.

This book is intended to present the principal approaches to asset allocation from the perspective of a practitioner. Hence we present the underlying theory intuitively, and we limit the mathematics to that which is necessary for application or exposition (which fortunately is of great convenience for the author). Moreover, we have taken considerable care to present these approaches objectively, focusing not only on their merits but their limitations as well. In fact, the reader may detect an undertone of cynicism, which merely reflects a conscious effort not to sell one approach or the other.

In addition to presenting an objective description of the principal approaches to asset allocation, this book attempts to dispel some of the common misperceptions about asset allocation, for example, the notion that Treasury bills reduce a pension fund's risk or the idea that tactical asset allocation is predominantly prospective. Moreover, this book attempts to cut through much of the superficial complexities of asset allocation by concentrating on the essence of the various strategies.

The book is organized as follows. Part 1 focuses on the principal approaches to asset allocation. Chapter 1 addresses strategic asset allocation, including the theoretical motivation and the mathematics necessary for application. Following the same format, Chapter 2 describes dynamic hedging strategies for asset allocation, while Chapter 3 deals with tactical asset allocation. Chapter 4 attempts to unify these three approaches conceptually by comparing and contrasting them within the familiar framework of payoff diagrams. Part 1 is concluded with a short story intended to illustrate the application of strategic asset allocation in a real world setting.

Part 2 deals with important innovations to asset allocation. In 1986, the Financial Accounting Standards Board promulgated changes in the rules for valuing and disclosing corporate pension liabilities. Hence Chapter 5 shows how to modify strategic asset allocation to incorporate pension liabilities, while Chapter 6 addresses the same issue with respect to dynamic hedging strategies. In light of the enormous shift toward global diversification, Chapter 7 discusses the impact of foreign exchange risk in asset allocation strategies, and it presents a simple algorithm for efficiently hedging foreign exchange risk. Part 2 also concludes with a short story dealing with the issue of liabilities in asset allocation decisions.

Part 3 addresses procedural issues surrounding asset allocation. Chapter 8 addresses the problem of estimating the inputs required to implement asset allocation strategies, focusing both on historical data and forecasting methods. Chapter 9 deals with execution, with emphasis on the use of derivative instruments. Chapter 10 focuses on the evaluation of asset allocation strategies. In keeping with the tone of the book, this chapter attempts to expose some of the statistical techniques that are used (unwittingly, of course) to misrepresent the expected or actual contribution of asset allocation strategies. Again, we conclude the part with a short story intended to highlight some of the notions presented in these chapters.

The book also includes four technical appendices to assist those who wish to apply the strategies presented in the book.

Most of the ideas presented in this book are based on the original contributions of other researchers. Naturally, we have taken great care to present and to attribute these ideas accurately. As such, we owe a great debt to those authors whose names are scattered throughout the footnotes.

In addition, several friends have read and commented on this book, including John Manley and Neil McCarthy. Their comments have improved the presentation significantly, but of course, they are not responsible for any remaining errors. Finally, a special thanks is due to Pamela Ward, who helped considerably with much of the statistical analysis and with the preparation of the exhibits.

Mark P. Kritzman

CONTENTS

*Common sense is the last refuge
of the unenlightened.*

PART 1

THE PRINCIPAL APPROACHES

The purpose of Part 1 is to describe in some detail the methodology involved in performing the three principal approaches to asset allocation.

Chapter 1 presents strategic asset allocation, which addresses the efficient combination of asset classes that is consistent with an investor's willingness to incur risk in order to increase expected return. Strategic asset allocation is based on portfolio theory, which was introduced initially to address the combination of individual securities into efficiently diversified portfolios. The principal focus of strategic asset allocation is to identify the asset mix that will yield the optimal balance between expected return and risk for a relatively long investment horizon. Implicit in the choice of a particular asset mix is the assumption that we will not alter the asset class weights.

Dynamic hedging strategies, which are presented in Chapter 2, protect a portfolio from market declines, while preserving the opportunity to participate in market advances. In order to achieve this protection, a portfolio's asset mix must be changed regularly as its value rises and falls. Portfolio insurance, the most common dynamic hedging strategy, is based on the arbitrage arguments that underlie the valuation of options. From option valuation theory we know that we can produce the same conditional payoff as a put option by selling a fraction of the underlying risky asset short and lending at the riskless rate. We can replicate a protective put option strategy by adding these positions to investment in the risky asset. This equivalence implies that we can protect a portfolio by varying its exposure between a risky asset and a riskless asset.

Chapter 3 deals with tactical asset allocation. Whereas dynamic hedging strategies require continual revision of a portfolio's asset mix to protect it from market declines, tactical asset allocation requires continual revision of a portfolio's asset mix to exploit transitory misvaluations among asset classes. Hence, the focus of tactical asset allocation is to enhance return rather than to control risk. The central notion of tactical asset allocation is mean reversion. This notion, in its simplest form, refers to the phenomenon in which prices fluctuate around an equilibrium value that serves as an anchor or central tendency. The implicit assumption of mean reversion is that markets frequently overcompensate for changes in fundamental value usually because investors become more risk tolerant as prices rise and more risk averse as prices fall.

The final chapter of Part 1 employs a pedagogical device known as a payoff diagram to reveal the essence of the principal asset allocation strategies. This framework illustrates that dynamic hedging strategies tend to perform well when holding period returns among asset classes diverge significantly, whereas tactical asset allocation strategies usually generate superior results when asset class values vibrate within a relatively narrow interval.

CHAPTER 1

STRATEGIC ASSET ALLOCATION

INTRODUCTION

In March 1952, Harry Markowitz published an article entitled "Portfolio Selection"[1] which describes how to combine assets into efficiently diversified portfolios. This landmark article, which was based on an earlier work by John Von Neumann and Oscar Morgenstern,[2] established the theoretical foundation for what is now known as *portfolio theory*. Although portfolio theory was developed to address diversification among individual securities, it serves as the basis for strategic asset allocation decisions.

The important assumptions that underlie portfolio theory are straightforward:

- Investors are rational in the sense that they wish to maximize the expected utility of their investment.
- In so doing, they choose investments according to their expected return and risk.
- Rational investors prefer more return to less return and less risk to more risk.
- Return is defined as income plus price change expressed as a percentage of beginning price.
- Risk is defined as uncertainty, which is reflected by variability around the expected return.

From these assumptions, Markowitz prescribed a rule for selecting investments called the *expected return-variance maxim (E-V maxim)*. This rule states that investors should choose portfolios with the highest level of expected return at each level of variance. The E-V maxim underscores the normative nature of portfolio theory in that it describes how investors should behave, not necessarily how they actually do behave.

In fact, in formulating his theory for portfolio selection, Markowitz observed an important oversight in how investors typically choose investment portfolios. Investors failed to account correctly for the covariance among security returns. Markowitz showed that the risk of a securities portfolio is not necessarily equal to the average risk of the component securities. The important difference is the covariance among the securities. Securities whose prices tend to change in concert do not offer as much opportunity to reduce a portfolio's risk below the average risk of the component securities as do securities whose prices tend to change independently of each other. Securities whose prices tend to change inversely with each other offer the most opportunity to reduce portfolio risk.

Moreover, Markowitz showed that securities can be combined into efficiently diversified portfolios such that, at a given level of risk, there are no other portfolios that offer the same expected return or a higher expected return. Markowitz referred to these portfolios as *efficient portfolios*. A continuum of efficient portfolios can be traced in dimensions of expected return and risk to form what is called the *efficient frontier*. Markowitz's insights about efficient diversification, although originally discussed in the context of weighting individual securities, are equally applicable in the context of combining asset classes such as stocks and bonds.

THE MATHEMATICS OF PORTFOLIO THEORY

In order to apply portfolio theory to asset allocation, we must first compute expected return and risk for each asset class as well as the relationship between the returns of each pair of asset classes.

Return

Return is a straightforward concept. It is defined as the income generated by an asset, plus or minus any price change that occurs over the holding period, all divided by the asset's price at the start of the period.

For common stock, return equals:

$$\frac{\text{Dividends} + (\text{Ending price} - \text{Beginning price})}{\text{Beginning price}}$$

For bonds, we simply substitute interest income for dividends:

$$\frac{\text{Interest income} + (\text{Ending price} - \text{Beginning price})}{\text{Beginning price}}$$

In general, we can express return as shown in Formula 1–1.

Formula Formula 1–1   Return

$$R = \frac{(I + E - B)}{B}$$

where

R = Return
I = Income
E = Ending price
B = Beginning price

Expected return is the estimate of return for which there is a 50 percent chance of experiencing an actual return that is either above or below the estimated return. Estimates of expected return are often based on the distribution of past returns or on more subjective considerations usually involving economic forecasts. We can summarize expected return as shown in Formula 1–2.

Formula 1–2   Expected Return

$$\hat{R} = \sum_{i=1}^{n} (R_i \cdot P_i)$$

where

$\hat{R}$ = Expected return
R_i = Observed return i

P_i – Probability of occurrence of return i

n = Number of observed returns

It is trivial to calculate the expected return for a combination of assets. It is simply the weighted average of the component assets' expected returns.

Suppose we estimate the expected return of stocks as 15 percent and the expected return of bonds as 10 percent. If we construct a portfolio that is invested 60 percent in stocks and 40 percent in bonds, the expected return of this portfolio is 13 percent, so long as we do not change the allocations.

$$(15\% \cdot 60\%) + (10\% \cdot 40\%) = 13\%$$

We can also obtain this result by computing the terminal value of $60 invested at 15 percent and $40 invested at 10 percent. The $60 investment grows to $69, while the $40 investment grows to $44. The sum of these investments is $113, exactly 13 percent greater than the total initial investment of $100.

Thus, we can express the expected return for a portfolio of assets as shown in Formula 1–3

Formula 1–3   Portfolio Expected Return

$$R_p = \sum_{i=1}^{n} (R_i \cdot W_i)$$

where

R_p = Expected return of portfolio

n = Number of assets in portfolio

R_i = Expected return of asset i

W_i = Percent invested in asset i

Risk

Risk is a slightly more complicated concept, especially for a group of assets. Risk is based on the notion of uncertainty. The less certain we are that an asset's actual return will be close to its expected return, the more risk that asset carries. For example, if two assets both have an expected return of 10 percent, but two thirds of the time one asset's actual returns fall within a range of 8 to 12 percent and the other asset's actual returns fall within a range of 0 to 20 percent, the second asset is riskier.

Statistically, risk is measured by the *standard deviation* of returns, which shows the dispersion of the actual returns around the average return. This is best illustrated by an example. The Standard & Poor's 500 Stock Average generated the following annual returns over the 10 years ended in 1987.

1978	6.56%	1983	22.51%
1979	18.44%	1984	6.27%
1980	32.42%	1985	32.16%
1981	−4.91%	1986	18.77%
1982	21.41%	1987	5.25%

If we sum these returns and divide by 10, we find that the average return for this period was 15.89 percent. To compute the standard deviation, we must first compute the difference between each annual return and the average return. Since the average of these differences, by construction, is 0, we square each difference, sum these values, and divide by 9 (10–1)[3] to get the average squared difference. This value is called the *variance* of the returns. Since the variance is computed from squared values, it is not expressed in the same units as the annual returns. To convert the variance to the same units as the annual returns, we take its square root. This value equals the standard deviation of the returns. These computations are carried out in Table 1–1.[4]

The average of the squared differences between each return and the average return equals the variance of the returns (1.50%), and the square root of the variance equals the standard deviation of returns (12.26%). These calculations can be summarized by Formulae 1–4 and 1–5:

Formula 1–4 Variance

$$V = \frac{\sum_{i=1}^{n} (R_i - \bar{R})^2}{n - 1}$$

TABLE 1–1
Variance and Standard Deviation

Year	Return	Difference from Average	Squared Difference
1978	6.56%	−9.33%	0.87%
1979	18.44%	2.55%	0.07%
1980	32.42%	16.53%	2.73%
1981	−4.91%	−20.80%	4.33%
1982	21.41%	5.52%	0.30%
1983	22.51%	6.63%	0.44%
1984	6.27%	−9.62%	0.93%
1985	32.16%	16.27%	2.65%
1986	18.77%	2.89%	0.08%
1987	5.25%	−10.64%	1.13%
Average	15.89%	0.00%	1.50%
Square root			12.26%

Formula 1–5   Standard Deviation

$$S = \sqrt{\frac{\sum_{i=1}^{n} (R_i - \bar{R})^2}{n - 1}}$$

where

V = Variance of returns

S = Standard deviation of returns

R_i = Return in period i

$\bar{R}$ = Average return

n = Number of periods

To compute the standard deviation of a combination of assets, we must account for the interaction between each pair of assets. If assets are similarly influenced by factors that cause prices to change, their returns will be closely linked. For example, when some Latin American governments defaulted on their debt obligations to U.S. money center banks in

1987, the stock prices of those banks dropped almost in unison. Similarly, since bank earnings are highly sensitive to changes in interest rates, their stock prices tend to rise or fall as interest rates change. As a consequence, the standard deviation of a diversified portfolio of money center bank stocks is not much lower than the average standard deviation of the component stocks, since their returns are tied to each other.

On the other hand, by combining airline stocks and energy stocks, we can reduce a portfolio's standard deviation significantly below the average standard deviation of the component assets. Since airline profits are sensitive to fuel costs, these stocks tend to perform poorly when oil prices rise, but they do well when oil prices fall. Most energy companies, conversely, enjoy higher profits when oil prices rise, while they experience declining profits as oil prices fall. Hence, these groups of stocks, when combined in a portfolio, tend to offset each other's returns, at least to the extent oil prices change, thereby reducing the variability of returns in the entire portfolio.

Markowitz formalized this notion in his classic article, "Portfolio Selection."[5] He showed that the standard deviation of a portfolio of assets depends, in part, on the extent to which the assets' returns co-vary.

Covariance between two assets equals the product of their standard deviations times their correlation coefficient. The _correlation coefficient_ measures the association between the returns of assets, and it ranges in value from +1 to –1.

A correlation coefficient of 1 implies that the returns of the assets move in lockstep with each other, although not necessarily by equal increments. For example, if we purchase a portfolio of stock index futures on margin (that is, we borrow funds to cover half the value of the portfolio), the returns of this leveraged portfolio will change two units for every one unit change in the returns of the underlying stock index. Although changes in the returns of our portfolio and the underlying stock index will differ by a factor of 2, they will have a correlation coefficient of 1.

A correlation coefficient of –1 implies that returns change inversely with each other with perfect predictability. Of course, the absolute value of the magnitude of the changes need not be the same. For example, a portfolio that consists of cash and a short position in stock index futures will be perfectly inversely correlated with the underlying stock index, yet its value will change by smaller increments than will the underlying stock index.

If the correlation coefficient equals 0, the returns are uncorrelated with each other. It is tempting to assume that they move independently of each other, but in a strict sense, this assumption is false. Even if the returns of two assets have a correlation coefficient of 0, it is possible that by transforming their returns to different units they may exhibit some interdependence.

The correlation coefficient between two series of asset returns can be expressed as shown in Formula 1–6.

Formula 1–6   Correlation Coefficient

$$r_{1,2} = \frac{\displaystyle\sum_{i=1}^{n} (R_{1i} - \bar{R}_1) \cdot (R_{2i} - \bar{R}_2)}{\sqrt{\displaystyle\sum_{i=1}^{n} (R_{1i} - \bar{R}_1) \cdot \sum_{i=1}^{n} (R_{2i} - \bar{R}_2)}}$$

where

$r_{1,2}$ = Correlation coefficient between asset 1 and asset 2

R_{1i} = Return of asset 1 in period i

$\bar{R}_1$ = Average return of asset 1

R_{2i} = Return of asset 2 in period i

$\bar{R}_2$ = Average return of asset 2

n = Number of periods

This formula, at first glance, may not have much intuitive appeal (or any kind of appeal, for that matter). If we examine this formula, however, some obvious properties of the correlation coefficient are apparent.

For example, if asset 1's returns tend to be greater than its average return when asset 2's returns are greater than its average return, the correlation coefficient will be positive. We can also observe that the correlation coefficient will be positive if asset 1's returns are less than its average return when asset 2's returns are less than its average return. These observations should comport with our intuition, since we know that the correlation coefficient is positive when asset returns move together.

Conversely, we can observe that if asset 1's returns are greater than its average return when asset 2's returns are less than its average return, the correlation coefficient will be negative. Similarly, the correlation coefficient will be negative if asset 1's returns are less than its average return when asset 2's returns tend to be greater than its average return. This observation makes sense, since when asset returns move opposite to each other they are negatively correlated.

Figure 1–1 depicts the relationship between two assets whose returns are perfectly positively correlated with each other and whose standard deviations are equal to each other.

Figure 1–2 depicts the opposite situation; the returns of the two assets are perfectly negatively correlated and the assets have the same standard deviations.

Figure 1–3 shows the relationship between two assets whose returns are uncorrelated with each other.

Finally, Figure 1–4 shows the relationship between two assets whose

FIGURE 1–1
Correlation Coefficient = +1

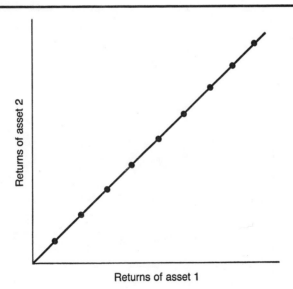

returns are positively, but not perfectly, correlated with each other and whose standard deviations are not equal. (In this illustration, asset 2 has a higher standard deviation than does asset 1.)

Although the correlation coefficient measures the direction and the degree of association between asset returns, it is an inadequate description of covariance, since it ignores the magnitude of each asset's variability.

In order to measure the covariance between assets, it is necessary to consider the relative volatility of their returns as well as the degree to which their returns are associated with each other. Specifically, covariance bewteen two assets can be expressed as shown in Formula 1–7.[6]

Formula 1–7   Covariance

$$C = S_1 \cdot S_2 \cdot r_{1,2}$$

FIGURE 1–2
Correlation Coefficient = –1

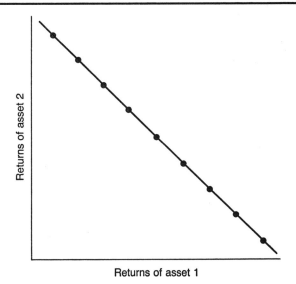

Returns of asset 1

FIGURE 1–3
Correlation Coefficient = 0

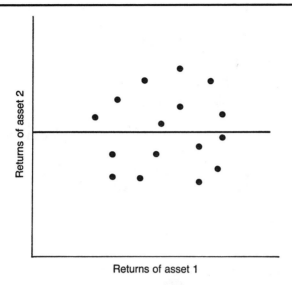

Returns of asset 2

Returns of asset 1

FIGURE 1–4
Positive Correlation Coefficient with Unequal Standard Deviations

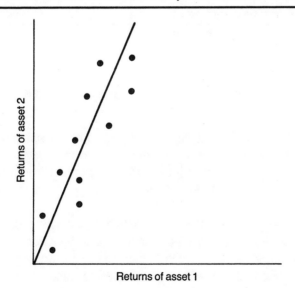

Returns of asset 2

Returns of asset 1

where

C = Covariance between two assets
S_1 = Standard deviation of asset 1
S_2 = Standard deviation of asset 2
$r_{1,2}$ = Correlation coefficient between asset 1 and asset 2

We are now ready to compute the standard deviation of a portfolio of assets. We will start with a simple case of two assets.

The standard deviation of returns for a portfolio of two assets can be expressed as shown in Formula 1–8.[mp,.5p0]

Formula 1–8   Portfolio Standard Deviation

$$S_p = \sqrt{\underbrace{\left(S_1^2 \cdot W_1^2\right)}_{STOCKS} + \underbrace{\left(S_2^2 \cdot W_2^2\right)}_{BONDS} + 2 \underbrace{\left(r_{1,2}\right)}_{\substack{CORRELATION \\ .30 \\ Ace\ p\ 53}} \cdot \underbrace{\left(S_1 \cdot W_1\right)}_{STOCKS} \cdot \underbrace{\left(S_2 \cdot W_2\right)}_{BONDS}}$$

where

S_p = Standard deviation of portfolio
STOCK S_1 = Standard deviation of asset 1 σ_1
BONDS S_2 = Standard deviation of asset 2 σ_2
60? W_1 = Percent invested in asset 1 x_i
40? W_2 = Percent invested in asset 2 x_i
±1 $r_{1,2}$ = Correlation coefficient between asset 1 and asset 2

As can be seen from Formula 1–8, a portfolio's standard deviation depends to a great extent on the correlation between assets.

The impact of the correlation coefficient on the relationship between a portfolio's expected return and its standard deviation is illustrated in Figure 1–5.

Figure 1–5 shows that, if two assets are perfectly positively correlated, it is not possible to reduce the standard deviation of a portfolio consisting of these two assets below the weighted average of the component assets' standard deviations. On the other hand, if two assets are perfectly inversely correlated, it is possible to find some combination of

FIGURE 1–5
Correlation Coefficient and Portfolio Risk

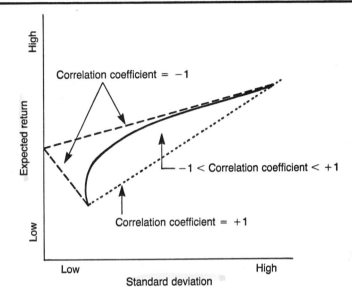

those two assets that will completely eliminate portfolio risk. (For example, if the component assets have equal standard deviations, a 50 percent allocation to each asset will eliminate portfolio risk.) The distance, moving right to left, of the curved line and the kinked line from the straight line reflects the degree to which portfolio risk can be reduced for a given level of expected return by virtue of the fact that the component assets' returns are less than perfectly positively correlated.

Thus far we have restricted our discussion of portfolio risk to portfolios with only two assets. As we increase the number of assets under consideration, it becomes computationally more cumbersome to estimate a portfolio's standard deviation. Consider a three-asset portfolio. Not only must we estimate each asset's standard deviation, but we must also estimate three covariances: the covariance of asset 1 and asset 2, the covariance of asset 1 and asset 3, and the covariance of asset 2 and asset 3. As the number of assets in the portfolio increases, the number of covariances that we must estimate increases at a higher rate. In general, the number of covariances that we need to estimate in order to compute a portfolio's standard deviation is given by Formula 1–9.[7]

Formula 1–9   Number of Covariances

$$n_c = \frac{n \cdot (n - 1)}{2}$$

where

n_c = Required number of covariances to estimate a portfolio's standard deviation

n = Number of assets in the portfolio

The standard deviation of a three-asset portfolio is computed as shown in Formula 1–10.

Formula 1–10   Standard Deviation of Three-Asset Portfolio

$$S_p = \sqrt{\begin{aligned} & S_1^2 \cdot W_1^2 + S_2^2 \cdot W_2^2 + S_3^2 \cdot W_3^2 + \\ & 2 \cdot r_{1,2} \cdot S_1 \cdot W_1 \cdot S_2 \cdot W_2 + \\ & 2 \cdot r_{1,3} \cdot S_1 \cdot W_1 \cdot S_3 \cdot W_3 + \\ & 2 \cdot r_{2,3} \cdot S_2 \cdot W_2 \cdot S_3 \cdot W_3 \end{aligned}}$$

where

S_p = Portfolio standard deviation

S_1 = Standard deviation of asset 1

S_2 = Standard deviation of asset 2

S_3 = Standard deviation of asset 3

W_1 = Percent invested in asset 1

W_2 = Percent invested in asset 2

W_3 = Percent invested in asset 3

$r_{1,2}$ = Correlation coefficient between asset 1 and asset 2

$r_{1,3}$ = Correlation coefficient between asset 1 and asset 3

$r_{2,3}$ = Correlation coefficient between asset 2 and asset 3

The Efficient Frontier

In the preceding pages, we describe how to compute the expected return and standard deviation of a portfolio of assets, but we have yet to describe how to select the so-called optimal portfolio. Our next task in our search for the optimal portfolio is to distinguish those portfolios which are efficient from those which are inefficient.

Portfolio theory defines an *efficient portfolio* as one that offers the highest level of expected return for a given level of risk. It also can be defined as one that minimizes risk for a given level of expected return. If we were to plot every portfolio that could be formed from the assets under consideration in dimensions of expected return and risk, and we were to trace a line connecting all of the efficient portfolios, this line would form the efficient frontier. Rational investors would restrict their choice of a portfolio to those portfolios that appeared on the efficient frontier. Figure 1–6 shows the efficient frontier, together with a portfolio that is inefficient.

Portfolio 1 at the left extreme of the efficient frontier offers relatively low expected return, but this return is highly reliable since portfolio 1 has very low risk. If the component assets were stocks, bonds, and short-term securities, portfolio 1 typically would be heavily weighted toward short-term securities. Portfolio 2 offers a higher expected return than portfolio 1, but its return is less certain, as evidenced by its higher standard deviation. This portfolio would typically include some stocks and bonds along with short-term securities. Portfolio 3 at the right extreme of the efficient frontier offers the highest expected return, but it also exposes the investor to the most risk. This portfolio would be invested entirely in the asset with the highest expected return, which typically would be stocks. Portfolio 4, plotted below the efficient frontier, is inefficient and, therefore, undesirable, since we could increase expected return without incurring additional risk by moving up to portfolio 2 on the efficient frontier. Alternatively, if the expected return of portfolio 4 were sufficiently high given our required return, we could preserve the same level of expected return but incur less risk by moving left to portfolio 1 on the efficient frontier.

We would prefer a portfolio located above the efficient frontier, but no such portfolio exists, given our choice of asset classes and our assumptions about expected return and risk. Therefore, we can regard the efficient frontier as a constraint. It represents the best possible combinations of expected return and risk available for our consideration.

FIGURE 1–6
The Efficient Frontier

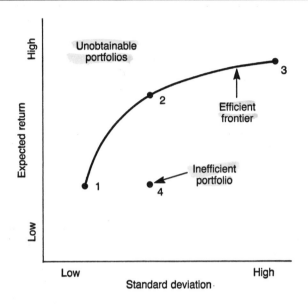

If we are restricted from selling an asset short, a portfolio consisting entirely of the riskiest asset always lies on the efficient frontier so long as it offers the highest expected return. However, the asset with the lowest level of risk does not lie on the efficient frontier, unless it is perfectly positively correlated with the other assets or unless it has no risk at all. Otherwise, it would be possible to combine the minimum-risk asset with another asset with which it is not perfectly positively correlated so as to produce a portfolio that has less risk and a higher expected return.

The following example demonstrates this point. Suppose there are only two assets for us to consider—stocks and bonds. Suppose that stocks have an expected return of 15 percent and a standard deviation of 20 percent, while bonds have an expected return of 10 percent and a standard deviation of 10 percent. Furthermore, suppose stock returns are 20 percent correlated with bond returns.

A portfolio consisting of 85 percent bonds and 15 percent stocks has an expected return of 10.75 percent (see Formula 1–3).

$$.10 \cdot .85 + .15 \cdot .15 = .1075$$

The standard deviation of this portfolio equals 9.56 percent (see Formula 1–8).

$$\sqrt{.10^2 \cdot .85^2 + .20^2 \cdot .15^2 + 2 \cdot .20 \cdot .10 \cdot .85 \cdot .20 \cdot .15} = .0956$$

In this example, bonds represent the minimum-risk asset with a standard deviation of 10 percent. Yet, a portfolio consisting of 85 percent bonds and 15 percent stocks has less risk (9.56 percent) than an all-bond portfolio, even though stocks are twice as risky as bonds. Moreover, this portfolio has a higher expected return (10.75 percent versus 10 percent) than an all-bond portfolio. Given these assumptions of expected return and risk (including correlation), an all-bond portfolio is inefficient.

Now let us consider the maximum-expected return asset. In this example stocks have the higher expected return (15 percent versus 10 percent). Although it is possible to reduce portfolio risk by blending stocks with bonds, we can only accomplish this risk reduction at the expense of lowering the expected return below 15 percent. In our example, an all-stock portfolio offers the highest expected return of all possible combinations of stocks and bonds at its risk level. Alternatively, given its expected return of 15 percent, there is no other combination of stocks and bonds that has less risk. Hence, an all-stock portfolio satisfies the criteria for inclusion on the efficient frontier.

In order to identify the actual asset weights that form the portfolios along the efficient frontier, we need to minimize portfolio variance at each level of expected return. This process may not be straightforward to those who are uncomfortable with calculus and matrix algebra. Hence, this material is set out in Appendix A.

Suppose that we are interested in allocating our fund between two assets: asset 1, which has an expected return of 12 percent and a standard deviation of 20 percent; and asset 2, which has an expected return of 8 percent and a standard deviation of 10 percent. Further, suppose that the returns of asset 1 and asset 2 are 15 percent correlated with each other. The minimum-risk combinations of these two assets for expected returns of 8 percent through 12 percent (assuming 1 percent intervals) are shown in Table 1–2.

Not all of these portfolios are efficient, however. Portfolio 1 has an expected return of 8 percent with a standard deviation of 10 percent, while portfolio 2 has a higher expected return of 9 percent with a lower standard deviation of 9.6 percent. Therefore, to identify the efficient set of portfolios, we can trace a line through the portfolios identified by our solutions for the asset weights, and truncate it where its slope approaches infinity. This demarcation is illustrated in Figure 1–7.

The Optimal Portfolio

After we have identified all of the efficient portfolios, our next task is to select the *optimal* portfolio; that is, the particular portfolio that we find most suitable. In theory, "most suitable" refers to the portfolio that maximizes our expected utility. In practice, however, expected utility can be somewhat amorphous.

Figure 1–8 portrays several hypothetical utility curves which reflect combinations of expected return and risk between which a hypothetical investor is indifferent. Of course, utility curves that are closer to the upper left corner are more desirable, but given a particular utility curve, an investor is indifferent between any points along that curve. Although the shape of the utility curve differs among investors according to their appetites for risk, in general, utility curves are convex (their slopes increase at an increasing rate).[8] Convexity merely reflects the fact that at low levels of expected return we are willing to incur greater risk to increase expected return than we are at high levels of expected return.

The optimal (most suitable) portfolio is the portfolio with a combination of expected return and risk that is located at the point of tangency

TABLE 1–2
Minimum-Risk Portfolios

Portfolio	1	2	3	4	5
Asset 1 percent	0%	25%	50%	75%	100%
Asset 2 percent	100%	75%	50%	25%	0%
Expected return	8.0%	9.0%	10.0%	11.0%	12.0%
Standard deviation	10.0%	9.6%	11.8%	15.6%	20.0%

FIGURE 1–7
Efficient Portfolios

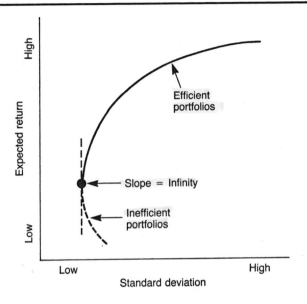

FIGURE 1–8
Utility Curves

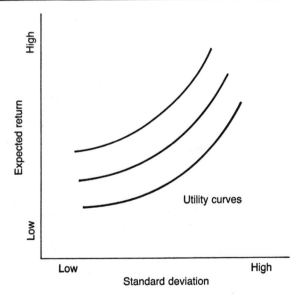

of expected return we are willing to incur greater risk to increase expected return than we are at high levels of expected return.

The optimal (most suitable) portfolio is the portfolio with a combination of expected return and risk that is located at the point of tangency between the efficient frontier and utility curve 2, as shown in Figure 1–9 (assuming utility curve 2 reflects our attitude toward risk and return). At this point our preference for exchanging expected return and risk matches the best available tradeoff. Clearly, we would prefer a combination of expected return and risk located along utility curve 3, but utility curve 3 is located in a region that is unobtainable, given our assumptions about expected return and risk and our choice of assets. (Remember, the efficient frontier is a constraint). Utility curve 1, on the other hand, is undesirable since it is dominated by many of the portfolios along the efficient frontier.

FIGURE 1–9
The Optimal Portfolio

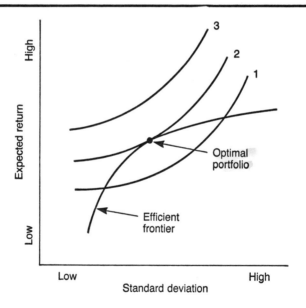

The analytics required to identify the theoretically optimal portfolio are similar to the process that we employed to isolate the efficient portfolios (see Appendix A). Within this context, though, our objective is to identify the efficient asset weights consistent with our willingness to incur incremental risk in order to achieve incremental expected return.

Although this approach is a useful paradigm for exposition, its practical value is questionable. How many of us can really determine which combinations of expected return and standard deviation are equally satisfying or, more likely, dissatisfying?

As an alternative to this utility theory approach, we can identify the optimal portfolio heuristically by evaluating the probable consequences of selecting various efficient portfolios. Since investment returns are approximately normally distributed, a portfolio's expected return and standard deviation are sufficient statistics for evaluating its entire range of outcomes.[9]

For example, suppose a portfolio has an expected return of 10 percent and a standard deviation of 12 percent. If returns are normally distributed, there is about a 2 in 3 chance that the actual return will fall within the range of plus or minus one standard deviation from the expected return; that is, the range of –2 percent to 22 percent. Moreover, there is about a 95 percent chance of experiencing a return between –14 percent and 34 percent (two standard deviations from the expected return). In fact, subject to estimation error, we can compute the probability of experiencing a return greater than or less than any target rate of return. This point is illustrated in Figure 1–10.

Figure 1–10 shows the familiar *normal distribution* (bell-shaped curve) for a portfolio with an expected return of 10 percent and a standard deviation of 12 percent. Exactly 50 percent of the area under this curve is to the right of the expected return, and the other 50 percent is to the left of the expected return. About 68 percent of the area under the curve falls between the two lines shown at –2 percent and 22 percent, which represents one standard deviation below and above the expected return. About 95 percent of the area under the curve falls between the two lines shown at –14 percent and 34 percent (two standard deviations from the expected return). Using these well-known properties of the normal distribution, simply by inspection we can infer the chance of experiencing returns above or below certain values, since area, within this context, is tantamount to likelihood of occurrence. For example, since 34 percent of the area falls

FIGURE 1–10
Portfolio Return Distribution

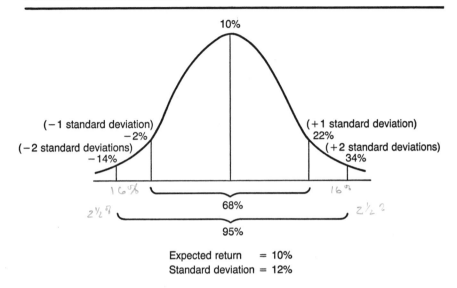

Expected return   = 10%
Standard deviation = 12%

between the expected return and the expected return plus one standard deviation, we know there is about a 16 percent chance of experiencing a return greater than 22 percent. By the same logic, we can infer that the likelihood of experiencing a return greater than −2 percent is about 84 percent. And, in like fashion, we can estimate the chance of experiencing a return of less than −14 percent to be only 2.5 percent. These inferences are possible because we know the extent of the area within one and two standard deviations of the expected return. However, we may not always be interested in returns that are exactly one or two standard deviations away from the expected return. For example, we may wish to know the likelihood that this portfolio's return will exceed 8.5 percent. To do so, we must first standardize the difference between 8.5 percent and the expected return of 10 percent by dividing it by the standard deviation of 12 percent.

$$\frac{8.5 - 10.0}{12.0} = -0.125$$

This calculation tells us that 8.5 percent is −0.125 standard deviations away from the expected return of 10 percent. In general, we can compute the number of standard deviations from the expected return as shown in Formula 1–11.

Formula 1–11   Number of Standard Deviations from Expected Return

$$z = \frac{T - R}{S}$$

where

z = Number of standard deviations from expected return

T = Target return

R = Portfolio expected return

S = Portfolio standard deviation

To find the area under the curve to the right of 8.5 percent (chance of exceeding) or to the left of 8.5 percent (chance of not exceeding), we simply locate the z value in a normal distribution table. These tables are found in most elementary statistics books. We must be careful, though. Some tables show the cumulative area to the left of the z value.

In this case, $N[z]$ (the value in the table) equals the area to the left of the target return, that is, the chance of failing to exceed the target return. If z equals −0.125, the corresponding probability is 45 percent. $1 - N[z]$, therefore, equals the chance of exceeding the target return, which is 55 percent for the case where z equals −0.125.

Some tables, however, show the area between the z value and the expected value. In this case, the chance of failing to exceed the target return equals $.5 + N[z]$, while the chance of exceeding the target return equals $.5 - N[z]$.

The values in the normal distribution table are determined by integrating the normal distribution function. Since this exercise poses somewhat of a challenge to many of us, an alternative method (in the absence of a table) is to estimate these values using a numerical approximation procedure. A cumulative normal distribution table and a numerical approximation procedure are included in Appendix B and Appendix C, respectively.

These probability estimates pertain to an annual investment horizon, assuming our estimates of expected return and risk are annualized values. However, we may be interested in the likelihood of exceeding a particular return *on average* over a multiple-year horizon. If our estimates of expected return and standard deviation are appropriate estimates for each of the years within the multiple-year horizon and the returns are independent of each other from year to year, then we can estimate the likelihood of exceeding some target return on average over several years as $1 - N[z_n]$. The method for determining the number of standard deviations from the expected return is set out in Formula 1–12.

Formula 1–12   Multiple-Year Number of Standard Deviations from Expected Return

$$z_n = \frac{T - R}{S / \sqrt{n}}$$

where

   z_n = Number of standard deviations from expected return
   T = Annualized target return
   R = Annualized portfolio expected return
   S = Annualized portfolio standard deviation
   n = Number of years in investment horizon

From Formula 1–12, it is apparent that if the expected return exceeds the target return, the chance of experiencing a return greater than the target will increase as the length of the investment horizon increases. Of course, if the target return exceeds the expected return, the opposite is true. This fact simply reflects the notion that risk can be diversified across time because short-term outcomes tend to offset each other.

It may be the case that we are not interested in the probability of exceeding our target in any one year or on average over several years. Rather, we may wish to know the chance that we will exceed our target in every one of the years within our multiple-year investment horizon. This objective is equivalent to not falling short of our target in one or more of the interim years. Again, if we assume that year-to-year returns are independent of each other, we can estimate the likelihood of meeting our target two years in a row as the chance of meeting it in the first year times the chance of meeting it in the second year. Thus, if there is a 55 percent chance of meeting our target in any one of the two years, the chance of meeting our target two years consecutively is 55 percent squared, or 30 percent. In general, the confidence that we have in meeting or exceeding a target in each and every year of a multiple-year horizon is given by Formula 1–13.

Formula 1–13   Each–And–Every–Year Probability Estimate

$$P' = P^n$$

where

P' = Probability of exceeding target return each and every year of multiple-year horizon

P = Probability of exceeding target return in any one year of a multiple-year horizon

n = Number of years in investment horizon

We must be careful not to misrepresent the chance of failing to meet our target return in one or more of several years. It *does not* equal the probability of failure in any one year raised to the power of the number of years. Instead, it equals one minus the chance of meeting it in any one year raised to the power of the number of years ($1 - P^n$). For example, we showed earlier that if the chance of meeting our target in one year is 55 percent, the chance of meeting it two consecutive years equals 30 percent. Therefore, the chance of failure in one or more of the two years equals 1 − 30 percent, or 70 percent. This value does not equal the chance of failure in any one year squared, which in this example is 20 percent. The logic here is straightforward. We know that an "each and every year requirement" is more stringent than an "any one year requirement"; hence the chance of success must decrease while the chance of failure must increase.

The preceding probability analysis provides a framework for selecting the most satisfying portfolio by evaluating the likelihood that alternative portfolios will exceed or fail to exceed target returns that we deem critical.

SUMMARY

- Strategic asset allocation, which is based on the principles of port-folio theory, is the most common approach used to establish long-term asset mix guidelines.
- The key insight of portfolio theory is that the risk of a portfolio of assets is typically lower than the average risk of the component assets.
- Portfolios that offer the highest level of expected return for a given level of risk (standard deviation) are called efficient portfolios, and a continuum of such portfolios plotted in dimensions of expected return and risk is called the efficient frontier.
- The optimal portfolio for a particular investor is located at the point along the efficient frontier that is tangent to that investor's utility curve.
- A utility curve measures the rate at which an investor is willing to incur an incremental unit of risk in order to increase expected return by one unit.
- Since most investors cannot easily express the rate at which they are willing to incur additional risk to increase expected return, it is common to identify optimal portfolios by evaluating each efficient portfolio's likelihood of satisfying specified investment objectives.

NOTES

1. H. Markowitz, "Portfolio Selection," *Journal of Finance* (March 1952), pp. 77–91.
2. J. Von Neumann and O. Morgenstern, *Theory of Games and Economic Behavior* (Princeton University Press, 1944).
3. We divide by the number of observations less one because we have used up one degree of freedom in estimating the average return.
4. The approach we have described to estimate variance and standard deviation is an approximation. To be more precise, we should derive our estimates from returns that are calculated as the difference in the logarithms of the asset values.
5. Markowitz, "Portfolio Selection," pp. 77–91.
6. Covariance can also be expressed as the average value of:

$$(R_{1i} - \bar{R}_1) \times (R_{2i} - \bar{R}_2)$$

where

R_{1i} = Return of asset 1 in period i
$\bar{R}_1$ = Average return of asset 1
R_{2i} = Return of asset 2 in period i
$\bar{R}_2$ = Average return of asset 2

By expressing covariance in this form, it is apparent that the covariance of an asset with itself is its variance. Covariance increases in importance as the number of assets increases. In fact, for an equally weighted portfolio, as the number of assets approaches infinity, the variance of the portfolio approaches the average covariance between the component assets.

7. If we change this formula to $[n \cdot (n+1)] / 2$, it can be used to calculate the sum of $1 + 2 + 3 + \ldots + n$. In fact, there is an amusing story about this formula and the famous Swiss mathematician, Euler. According to legend, when Euler was a child just starting school the teacher asked the students in Euler's class to add the numbers from 1 to 100 so as to distract them for a while. After a few seconds, however, Euler raised his hand and said 5,050. The teacher asked Euler how he added the numbers so quickly. Euler described that he began by adding 1 plus 2 plus 3 but became bored. So he started again with 100 plus 99 plus 98. Then he noticed that 1 plus 100 equaled 101 as did 2 plus 99 and 3 plus 98. Thus, he realized that if he multiplied 100 by 101 and divided by 2 (so as not to double count) he would arrive at the answer.

8. Sometimes utility curves are depicted with expected return on the horizontal axis and risk on the vertical axis, in which case they are concave.

9. Actually, the logarithms of the wealth relatives of returns (that is, one plus the return) are normally distributed. This distinction is important over extended measurement periods such as five years or longer, but very little precision is lost if we assume that returns are normally distributed over short measurement periods.

CHAPTER 2

DYNAMIC HEDGING STRATEGIES

"A cat that sat on a hot stove once will not do so again."
Mark Twain

"Of course, neither will he sit on a cold stove."
Burton Malkiel

INTRODUCTION

Strategic asset allocation that is based on portfolio theory presumes, at least implicitly, that during the investment horizon investors will not change the asset mix they have selected unless they change one or more underlying assumptions. As an alternative to this "buy-and-hold" approach to asset allocation, many investors, particularly those with a short investment horizon, prefer a dynamic approach whereby they vary a fund's asset mix in order to generate a particular payoff pattern. This approach to asset allocation is referred to as a *dynamic hedging strategy*.

Perhaps the most well-known dynamic hedging strategy is portfolio insurance. *Portfolio insurance* is based on option valuation theory, yet it does not require investment in options. Instead we continually vary a portfolio's exposure to a risky asset and a riskless asset so as to ensure a prespecified minimum return while preserving the potential to participate in the gains of the risky asset. Under perfect market conditions, portfolio insurance generates the same outcome as a protective put option strategy.[1] The initial allocation to the risky and riskless assets, as well as the precise amount shifted as the portfolio's value changes through time, is based on the arbitrage arguments that underlie the valuation of options.

Although insurance on risky portfolios has been available intermittently since 1956, the option-based trading strategy widely referred to today as portfolio insurance was introduced in 1976 by Berkeley professors Hayne Leland and Mark Rubinstein.[2] The strategy was motivated, in part, by the simple fact that it is less costly to purchase an option on a portfolio than it is to purchase a portfolio of options on the component assets.

Consider a portfolio that consists of two assets, each of which is priced at $50 and has a standard deviation of 30 percent. Suppose that these two assets are uncorrelated with each other. Now suppose that we wish to protect this portfolio from declining below $95 by purchasing a put option on each asset with a strike price of $47.50. Let us assume that these options expire in one year and that the riskless rate of interest is 8 percent. If these options are priced fairly, it would cost us $3.04 for each option, resulting in a total cost of $6.08 to protect the portfolio from declining below $95. The value of these options is determined, in part, by the total risk of each of the underlying assets.

What if, instead of purchasing an option on each component asset, we could purchase an option on the total portfolio? How much would it cost us for the same level of protection? Since the assets are uncorrelated with each other, the total risk of the portfolio is less than the average risk of the component assets, since part of their risk is diversified away. To be exact, the portfolio's standard deviation is 21.21 percent.[3] A put option on the total portfolio with a strike price of $95 would provide the same level of protection, and this option would cost only $3.24. Hence, we can cut our cost nearly in half by purchasing an option on this portfolio rather than individual options on each of the component assets. This tradeoff is summarized in Table 2-1.

The problem with this strategy, of course, is that options on portfolios were not available in 1976 and, except for a few major indexes, are not available today. Hence, Leland and Rubinstein invented portfolio insurance to provide fairly priced protection for portfolios of risky assets.

TABLE 2-1
A Portfolio of Options versus an Option on a Portfolio

	Price	Standard Deviation	Strike Price	Put Price
Asset 1	$ 50.00	30.00%	$47.50	$3.04
Asset 2	$ 50.00	30.00%	$47.50	$3.04
Portfolio	$100.00	21.21%	$95.00	$3.24

THE MATHEMATICS OF DYNAMIC HEDGING STRATEGIES

As described earlier, portfolio insurance is a dynamic hedging strategy whereby we gradually shift a fund's exposure between a risky asset and a riskless asset so as to ensure a minimum return while preserving the potential to participate in possible gains from the risky asset. Before describing precisely how portfolio insurance works, it might be useful to define some relevant terms. Not surprisingly, some of the terms are analogous to insurance concepts. However, unlike conventional insurance, portfolio insurance is not based on the concept of pooling risk. Instead, it is based on the concept of arbitrage; hence, some of the terms also correspond to notions of option valuation.

In order to implement a portfolio insurance program, we must first specify a minimum value that we wish to protect the portfolio value from penetrating. This value is called the *floor*. It corresponds to the strike price in a protective put option strategy.

The *deductible* equals the difference between the initial portfolio value and the floor value. As in conventional insurance, the lower the deductible, the higher the cost of the protection.

The cost of a portfolio insurance strategy *ex ante* equals the price of a corresponding or "shadow" protective put option. After the fact, the cost of portfolio insurance equals the loss in return that occurs by not participating fully in the risky asset's return should it return more than the riskless return. In the context of conventional insurance, cost can be thought of as the insurance premium.

Upside capture refers to the percentage of the risky asset's terminal value that is captured by the insurance strategy, not the percentage of the risky asset's return. It equals the terminal value of the portfolio divided by the terminal value of the risky asset.

The *hedge ratio* equals the percentage of the portfolio that is allocated to the risky asset. It corresponds to *delta* in a protective put option strategy.

The *investment horizon* refers to the period over which the strategy is implemented. It corresponds to the time remaining until expiration in a protective put option strategy.

Some of these terms are illustrated in Figure 2–1, which shows the payoff functions for a risky asset and a portfolio insurance strate-

FIGURE 2–1
Portfolio Insurance Payoff Diagram

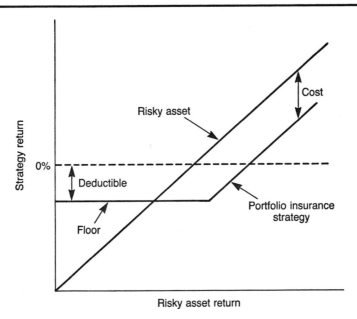

gy. A payoff function relates a strategy's return to the return of the risky asset. (See Chapter 4 for a more detailed discussion of payoff functions.)

Having defined some of the relevant terms of portfolio insurance, we will now demonstrate its correspondence to the theory of option valuation. As we mentioned earlier, portfolio insurance is equivalent to investment in a risky asset along with a protective put option. We will begin by demonstrating this equivalence within the framework of the binomial option pricing model. A protective put option strategy produces the same outcome that we could achieve by investing in a riskless asset along with a call option on a risky asset. Therefore, in the following section we will use the continuous-time Black-Scholes option pricing model to demonstrate how to implement a portfolio insurance strategy from this perspective.

PORTFOLIO INSURANCE USING THE
BINOMIAL MODEL

Suppose we wish to invest $100 so that it will capture the performance of a risky asset if it does well and at the same time lose no more than 5 percent should the risky asset perform poorly. We could achieve this outcome by investing in the risky asset along with a protective put option with a strike price of $95. Let us begin by deriving the value of a put option with a strike price of $95 on a risky asset that is valued at $100. For convenience, we will assume that this asset can either increase to $120 or decrease to $90. We will also assume that the riskless rate of interest is 8 percent. Figure 2–2 shows these possible outcomes in the familiar form of a binomial tree. The numbers in parentheses are the value of the put option given the possible prices for the risky asset. The possible values for the put option at expiration are obvious. They equal the maximum of zero or the strike price less the risky asset price. The value of the put option at the start of the tree is not as obvious.

We can replicate the payoff for a put option by selling short some fraction of the risky asset and lending some amount at the riskless rate of interest. We will demonstrate this equivalence shortly. In the meantime, we can use this equivalence to form two equations which, when solved simultaneously, will yield the specific amounts to sell short and to lend.

FIGURE 2–2
One-Period Binomial Tree

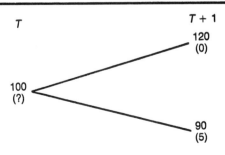

$$N \cdot 120.00 + 1.08 \cdot L = 0.00$$
$$N \cdot 90.00 + 1.08 \cdot L = 5.00$$

In the above equations, N equals the amount of the risky asset to sell short, while L equals the amount of money to lend at the riskless rate. It turns out that we can replicate the put option by selling short 16.67 percent of the risky asset and lending \$18.52 at 8 percent. Again, by virtue of the fact that we can replicate a put option by selling short the risky asset and lending at the riskless rate, we can determine the put option's value at the start of the period by summing our short position and the amount we lend, as shown below:

$$P = -.1667 \cdot 100 + 18.52 = 1.85$$

We can easily verify that selling short and lending in these amounts provides the same outcome as investment in a put option. For example, suppose the risky asset increases to \$120. The put option will expire with a net loss of \$1.85, the cost of the option. If, instead, we had sold short \$16.67 of the risky asset, we would have lost \$3.33. However, this loss would have been partly offset by lending \$18.52 at 8 percent, which would have generated \$1.48 in income, for a net loss of \$1.85, the same outcome as the put option strategy. Now suppose that the risky asset decreases to \$90. The option would have returned \$5. After subtracting its cost of \$1.85, we are left with a net gain of \$3.15. The short position of \$16.67 would have returned \$1.67. When added to the proceeds of lending \$18.52 at 8 percent, it too leaves a net gain of \$3.15.

Portfolio insurance, however, is not equivalent to a put option. Rather, it is intended to replicate investment in a risky asset together with a put option. Thus, to replicate a protective put option strategy, we simply add the investment in the risky asset to our short position, resulting in a net exposure of \$83.33 in the risky asset, as shown in Table 2–2.

There is only one problem with the strategy we have just described. In order to implement this strategy, we need \$101.85 (\$83.33 + \$18.52), but we only have \$100 to invest. If we intend to contain our potential loss to 5 percent by actually purchasing the risky asset along with the put option, we would have to scale back the amount of the risky asset that we purchase, such that when we add it to the cost of the put option, we would have spent exactly \$100. Otherwise the potential loss of \$5 on the strategy

TABLE 2–2
Option Replication

In Order to Replicate	Amount to Invest in Risky Asset	Amount to Lend
Put option	−16.67	18.52
Risky asset	100.00	0.00
Protective put option strategy	83.33	18.52

combined with the cost of the option could result in a total loss of more than 5 percent. In order to replicate this strategy by selling the risky asset short and lending at the riskless rate, we must first determine the precise combination of the risky asset and the put option that we wish to replicate. If we repeat the process described above, iteratively substituting various amounts for the risky asset, we will eventually find that we are able to purchase a put option valued at $2.78 to protect $97.22 of the risky asset. We can replicate the put option part of this strategy by selling 25.72 percent of the risky asset short (which equals $25) and lending $27.79 at the riskless rate. In Table 2–3, we again demonstrate that this strategy is equivalent to a put option.

In order to replicate a protective put option strategy, we add the $97.22 to the positions we established to replicate the put option, resulting in a $72.21 exposure to the risky asset and a $27.79 exposure to the riskless asset (which, of course, is tantamount to lending at the riskless rate).

The foregoing example is extremely oversimplified in the sense that it assumes the risky asset can only increase by 20 percent or decrease by 10 percent. We can overcome this simplification by including a greater number of intervals in our binomial tree. Alternatively, we can solve for the risky asset and riskless asset exposures by employing the Black-Scholes option pricing model.

PORTFOLIO INSURANCE USING THE BLACK-SCHOLES MODEL

As we mentioned earlier, portfolio insurance is a dynamic hedging strategy that replicates either investment in a risky asset along with a put option

TABLE 2–3
Strategy Payoffs

Risky asset return = 20%			
Put payoff:	0.00	Risky asset payoff: (−25 · .2)	−5.00
Put cost:	2.78	Lending payoff: (27.79 · .08)	2.22
Profit:	−2.78	Profit:	−2.78
Risky asset return = −10%			
Put payoff: (95 − .9 · 97.22)	7.50	Risky asset payoff: (−25 · −.1)	2.50
Put cost:	2.78	Lending payoff: (27.79 · .08)	2.22
Profit:	4.72	Profit:	4.72

(which we just demonstrated) or investment in a riskless asset along with a call option. In this section, we draw upon its correspondence to investment in a riskless asset plus a call option to show how the strategy can be implemented with the continuous-time Black-Scholes model.

Again, suppose we have $100 to invest and we want to be reasonably certain that we will have no less than $95 one year from now. Moreover, should the risky asset increase in value over the course of the year, we want to participate to the fullest extent possible. Let us assume that we can purchase a riskless asset to yield 8 percent and that the risky asset's standard deviation equals 20 percent. Let us start by computing the value of a call option on the risky asset. From the above information, we have all of the information required by the Black-Scholes model.

Risky asset value	$100
Strike price	$95
Risky asset standard deviation	.20
Riskless rate of return	.08
Time to expiration	1

The value of a call option under the Black-Scholes model is given by Formula 2–1.[4]

Formula 2–1 The Black-Scholes Model

$$C = R \cdot N(D) - Ke^{-rT} \cdot N(D - S \cdot \sqrt{T})$$

$$D = \frac{ln(R/K) + r + S^2/2) \cdot T}{S \cdot \sqrt{T}}$$

where

C = Value of call option
R = Value of risky asset
K = Strike price
r = Riskless rate of interest
S = Standard deviation of risky asset
T = Time remaining to expiration (years)
$N()$ = Cumulative normal density function
ln = Natural log
e = 2.7128 (constant)

First, let us proceed by computing the value for D as shown below.

$$D = \frac{ln(100/95) + (.08 + .2^2/2)}{.2} = .7565$$

Next, we substitute the value of D (.7565) into line 1 of Formula 2–1.

$$C = 100 \cdot N(.7565) - 95e^{-.08} \cdot N(.7565 - .2)$$
$$C = 100 \cdot N(.7565) - 87.6961 \cdot N(.5565)$$

If we look up the area under the normal distribution curve that corresponds to .7565 and .5565, we find that the value for this call option equals $15.17 ($100 · .7753 – $87.6961 · .7111). We can easily convert this call option value into a value for a put option by invoking the well-known relationship of put-call parity, which is shown in Formula 2–2.

Formula 2–2 Put-Call Parity

$$P = C - R + Ke^{-rT}$$

where

> P = Value of put option
> C = Value of call option
> R = Value of risky asset
> r = Riskless rate of interest
> T = Time remaining to expiration
> K = Strike price
> e = 2.7128 (constant)

According to Formula 2–2, the value of a put option, given the above parameters, equals $2.87 ($15.17 – $100 + $87.70). However, we are faced with the same problem that we encountered with the binomial model approach to portfolio insurance. The total cost of a protective put option strategy is greater than our available funds. We have only $100 to invest, but we need $100 to purchase the risky asset, plus an additional $2.87 to purchase the put option. Hence, we do not wish to replicate this particular strategy. Instead, we wish to replicate a protective put option strategy whereby we spend exactly $100. As we did earlier, we must iteratively change the amount of the risky asset until its value plus the cost of the shadow put option equals $100 exactly. Suppose we are lucky and on our next try we select $96.15 for our risky asset value. The value for D equals .5602, as shown below.

$$D = \frac{ln(96.15/95) + (.08 + .2^2/2)}{.2} = .5602$$

and the value for the call option equals $12.30.

$$C = 96.15 \cdot N(.5602) - 95e^{-.08} \cdot N(.5602 - .2)$$
$$C = 96.15 \cdot N(.5602) - 87.6961 \cdot N(.3602)$$
$$C = 96.15 \cdot .7123 - 87.6961 \cdot .6406 = 12.60$$

Again, using the put-call parity relationship, the value for a corresponding put option equals $3.85.

$$P = 12.60 - 96.15 + 87.70 = 3.85$$

Conveniently, the cost of a $3.85 put option used to protect a risky asset valued at $96.15 from declining below $95 exactly uses up our total available funds of $100. Therefore, our next task is to determine how to replicate this option strategy by investing in a risky and riskless asset.

Remember, in theory a portfolio insurance strategy is equivalent to investment in a risky asset along with a put option or investment in a riskless asset along with a call option. We will draw upon the latter correspondence to determine the initial positions for the risky and riskless assets. The letter D was not chosen arbitrarily in the Black-Scholes formula. $N(D)$ refers to *delta*, the fraction of the risky asset that hedges an investment in a call option on the risky asset. Therefore, in order to replicate a call option plus investment in a riskless asset (which is equivalent to replicating investment in a risky asset plus a put option), we simply invest an amount equal to *delta* times the risky asset in the risky asset, with the remainder of the fund allocated to the riskless asset. In the above example we would invest $68.48 (.7123 · $96.15) in the risky asset and the balance, $31.52, in the riskless asset.

Based on the above example, we can assign values to some of the portfolio insurance terms that we defined earlier. In our example, the floor equals $95, which corresponds to a minimum required return of –5 percent. The deductible, therefore, equals $5, the difference between the initial portfolio value and the floor value. The expected cost of this port folio insurance program equals $3.15, which, of course, is the cost of the shadow put option. Expected upside capture equals 96.15 percent, which can be viewed as the initial portfolio value less the cost of the shadow put option, all divided by the initial portfolio value. The initial hedge ratio equals 68.48 percent, the percent of the total portfolio that is allo cated to the risky asset at the start of the strategy. Finally, the investment horizon equals one year, the time remaining until the shadow protective put option expires.

As time passes and the value of the portfolio changes, we must adjust the risky and riskless asset positions according to the process that we have just described. (Of course, we no longer need to find the risky asset value by iteration, since it is whatever it is once the strategy begins.) As the portfolio's value rises, we increase its exposure to the risky asset, and we decrease its exposure to the risky asset as the portfolio's value declines (assuming the other inputs remain unchanged). In theory, we should re-balance the portfolio continuously, but continuous rebalancing is not possible. In practice, we must balance the cost of frequent trading with the imprecision that could result from infrequent trading in order to arrive at a reasonable trading rule.

Suppose that at the end of one year, the risky asset's total return is 20 percent and the portfolio's total return is 15.32 percent. In this case, experienced upside capture equals 96.10 percent (115.32/120.00), and the actual cost of the protection equals $3.90. This value could easily be greater than the value of the shadow put option at the beginning of the period for a variety of reasons. We would have incurred transaction costs in executing the strategy. If we used financial futures to execute the strategy, basis risk may have generated additional costs. Finally, the price of the portfolio may have changed quickly, not leaving us enough time to rebalance the portfolio to accord with the new hedge ratio.

If the risky asset instead declined by 20 percent, we should expect our portfolio to equal at least $95. Again, its value may be slightly greater or less than $95, to the extent our execution is less than perfect. We will address these issues and others in Chapter 9, which is devoted to execution.

CONSTANT PROPORTION PORTFOLIO INSURANCE

Portfolio insurance, as we have just described it, is plagued by several problems. First, by now it should be apparent that portfolio insurance is not particularly straightforward. Second, portfolio insurance is *time dependent*. That is, the strategy is implemented over a predefined investment horizon, and the hedge ratio at any point in time depends on the time remaining in our investment horizon. Its time dependence implies that we have an improbable attitude toward risk. For example, if, near the end of the investment horizon, the portfolio value is substantially above its floor value, it will be allocated almost entirely to the risky asset. If, on the other hand, it is at or below its floor value, it will be allocated almost entirely to the riskless asset. Now suppose that we wish to resume the strategy for another year. We must reallocate the portfolio according to the appropriate new hedge ratio, which will substantially change its riskiness. However, our attitude toward risk did not change. The change in the portfolio's riskiness is simply an artifact of the time dependence of portfolio insurance.

In 1986, at approximately the same time, André Perold[5] of Harvard and Fischer Black and Robert Jones[6] of Goldman Sachs introduced a dynamic hedging strategy called *constant proportion portfolio insurance* (CPPI), which addressed the two aforementioned limitations of traditional portfolio insurance. First of all, CPPI is extremely simple to understand and simple to implement. Secondly, CPPI is time invariant in the sense that it continues indefinitely and no trades are occasioned by the passage of time.

Here is how CPPI works. Suppose we have $100 to invest and we want to be certain of never having less than $85, yet we want to participate in the performance of a risky asset should it produce favorable returns. This type of objective should sound fairly familiar by now. The portfolio value equals $100 and the floor value equals $85. The difference between these two values is called the cushion, which in this case equals $15. Rather than deal with complicated option pricing formulae, we simply multiply the cushion by some value greater than one (the multiple) and allocate this amount to the risky asset and the balance to the riskless asset. As long as the portfolio's value does not decrease by more than the reciprocal of the multiple between revisions, the portfolio will never penetrate the floor. The CPPI investment rule is demonstrated in Table 2–4.

From Table 2–4, it is easy to see that CPPI increases the exposure to the risky asset as the portfolio's value rises, while it increases the exposure to the riskless asset as the portfolio's value falls. Moreover, as the portfolio falls in value, it becomes less and less sensitive to the performance of the risky asset since it is more heavily exposed to the riskless asset. A practical constraint of CPPI is that we would have to lever the portfolio if the portfolio value rose significantly above the floor value, which is not permitted for many institutional portfolios.

TABLE 2–4
Constant Proportion Portfolio Insurance

Floor = 85
Multiple = 5

Portfolio Value	Floor Value	Cushion	Risky Allocation	Riskless Allocation	Risky Return	Riskless Return
100.00	85.00	15.00	75.00	25.00	6.0%	0.6%
104.65	85.00	19.65	98.25	6.40	5.0%	0.6%
109.60	85.00	24.60	123.00	−13.40	−6.0%	0.6%
102.14	85.00	17.14	85.70	16.44	−7.0%	0.6%
96.24	85.00	11.24	56.20	40.04	−9.0%	0.6%
91.42	85.00	6.42	32.11	59.31		

An important limitation of CPPI as well as traditional portfolio insurance is that we are only protected from declines below a floor value that is indexed to the initial value of our portfolio. For example, if our portfolio were to increase sharply in the early part of our investment horizon and then subsequently fall, CPPI would not protect any of the gains we had experienced before the fall. If we were interested in protecting our gains, we could modify the strategy by defining the floor value as the higher of the previous floor value or some percentage of the portfolio's current value. Within this context, we can think of conventional CPPI as analogous to original cost insurance, while we can think of this modified strategy as analogous to replacement cost insurance. The replacement cost version of CPPI is shown in Table 2–5.

In the replacement cost version of CPPI, the floor value is continually reset as the portfolio value rises, thereby protecting some fraction of previous gains. In the above examples, this added protection was achieved at the cost of not participating as fully in the appreciation of the risky asset. Whereas the original cost version of CPPI achieved a return of 9.6 percent through the risky asset's appreciation, the replacement cost version achieved a slightly lower return of 8.7 percent. This loss in return was offset when the risky asset declined in value. Over the entire period, the original cost CPPI strategy lost 8.6 percent versus only 2.9 percent for the replacement cost strategy. Whether we prefer replacement cost protection

TABLE 2–5
Replacement Cost CPPI

Floor = maximum of previous floor value or 85 percent of new portfolio value
Multiple = 5

Portfolio Value	Floor Value	Cushion	Risky Allocation	Riskless Allocation	Risky Return	Riskless Return
100.00	85.00	15.00	75.00	25.00	6.0%	0.6%
104.65	88.95	15.70	78.49	26.16	5.0%	0.6%
108.73	92.42	16.31	81.54	27.19	−6.0%	0.6%
104.00	92.42	11.58	57.90	46.10	−7.0%	0.6%
100.22	92.42	7.80	39.02	61.20	−9.0%	0.6%
97.08	92.42	4.66	23.28	73.80		

or original cost protection depends on our particular attitude toward risk or other circumstances that may dictate one version or the other. In general, though, replacement cost protection is more conservative than original cost protection and, as we should expect, more expensive in terms of opportunity cost. It does have one unique advantage over original cost protection. Since the floor rises commensurately with the value of the portfolio, replacement cost CPPI never requires that we lever the portfolio (assuming, of course, that we did not start out levered).

SUMMARY

- We can protect a portfolio from falling below a prespecified value while preserving upside potential by following a dynamic hedging strategy called portfolio insurance.
- Portfolio insurance is designed to provide the same outcome as a protective put option strategy, yet it does not require investment in options. Instead, we shift a fund's mix toward a risky asset as the fund's value rises and toward a riskless asset as the fund's value declines.
- As an alternative to option replication, we can protect a portfolio by following a simpler dynamic hedging strategy called constant proportion portfolio insurance (CPPI).
- CPPI differs from traditional portfolio insurance in that the hedge ratio is not based on complicated option valuation theory and the hedge ratio in a CPPI strategy is invariant to the passage of time.

NOTES

1. A put option gives the purchaser the right (not obligation) to sell an asset at a specified price (strike price) on or before a specified date (expiration date). Therefore, we can combine put options with the underlying asset to ensure a minimum return on this combined investment.
2. H. Leland and M. Rubinstein, "The Evolution of Portfolio Insurance," in *Portfolio Insurance: A Guide to Dynamic Hedging,* ed. D. Luskin (New York: John Wiley & Sons, 1988), p. 54.

3. This value is computed as:

$$\sqrt{S_1{}^2 \cdot W_1{}^2 + S_2{}^2 \cdot W_2{}^2 + 2 \cdot r_{1,2} \cdot S_1 \cdot W_1 \cdot S_2 \cdot W_2}$$

where

S_1 = Standard deviation of asset 1

S_2 = Standard deviation of asset 2

W_1 = Percent invested in asset 1

W_2 = Percent invested in asset 2

$r_{1,2}$ = Correlation between asset 1 and asset 2

4. F. Black and M. Scholes, "The Pricing of Options and Corporate Liabilities," *Journal of Political Economy* 81 (May 1973), pp. 637–654.

5. A. Perold, "Constant Proportion Portfolio Insurance," *Harvard Business School Working Paper* (August 1986).

6. F. Black and R. Jones, "Simplifying Portfolio Insurance," *Goldman Sachs Research Report* (August 1986), p. 75.

CHAPTER 3

TACTICAL ASSET ALLOCATION

"A cynic is a man who knows the price of everything and
the value of nothing."

Oscar Wilde

INTRODUCTION

Thus far, we have presented strategic asset allocation, which presumes that
we buy and hold the asset mix that we selected at the beginning of our
investment horizon, and dynamic hedging strategies, which require us to
revise our asset mix in response to changes in our fund's value. In this
chapter, we introduce an alternative dynamic strategy called *tactical asset
allocation.*

As is true with dynamic hedging strategies, tactical asset allocation
requires that we revise our fund's asset mix periodically. Unlike a dynamic
hedging strategy, however, tactical asset allocation is proactive rather than
reactive. It is based on the presumption that we can improve a fund's
performance by investing in an asset class when it is undervalued, and
disinvesting in it when it is overvalued.

Proponents of tactical asset allocation might argue that investors who
accept the asset prices assigned by the market fit Oscar Wilde's definition
of a cynic, while those who practice tactical asset allocation properly
distinguish value from price.

There are perhaps as many approaches to tactical asset allocation as
there are practitioners of the strategy. Nonetheless, virtually all of these
approaches share the implicit assumption that asset price fluctuations
sometimes exaggerate fundamentally justified changes in asset values,

because investors typically become more risk tolerant as prices rise and less risk tolerant as prices fall.[1]

The process whereby asset prices fluctuate around some central tendency representing equilibrium coincides with a widely accepted notion called *mean reversion*. Although mean reversion has been documented in many states of nature and in numerous economic relationships, its application to asset pricing is vigorously disputed by many financial economists.[2] At the same time, other financial economists endorse the notion.[3] Before we investigate this controversy, let us review a simple example of mean reversion by considering the dynamics of oil prices. (We will ignore exogenous factors such as embargoes and war in our simple example.)

Let us begin with the assumption that oil prices are valued fairly, given current levels of supply and demand. As the population grows, consumption rises, leading to an increase in demand which eventually drives up the price of oil. Producers recognize that at higher prices it is profitable to drill additional wells and, at sufficiently high prices, to reopen previously capped wells to retrieve oil that was too expensive to extract at lower prices. Exploration increases and new technology is developed. Eventually, the pace of this activity leads to excessive production. Meanwhile, at higher prices, consumers become more conservation conscious and seek efficiencies and alternative sources of energy to reduce their dependency on oil. Eventually, the supply of oil exceeds the demand for it, and oil prices begin to decline. As prices fall, exploration slows, and the more expensive ventures to extract oil are no longer profitable at lower prices. Hence production falls until the demand for oil once again exceeds its supply and prices again rise. It is easy to see how these dynamics lead to a mean reverting process for oil prices.

The implicit assumption of those who promote tactical asset allocation is that the prices for asset classes such as stocks and bonds follow a similar mean reverting process (around equilibrium). Asset class prices fluctuate in anticipation of business cycle peaks and valleys, and these fluctuations are sometimes exaggerated by investor enthusiasm and fear.

The assumption of mean reversion in security prices, however, is quite controversial since financial theory depends to a large extent on the belief that prices follow a *random walk*. A mean reverting process, of course, is not random. If prices do, indeed, revert to an equilibrium value, and if we can estimate this value, then it follows that we can predict return.

This notion disturbs those who embrace classical finance because it implies that investment markets are inefficient. If investors knew, for example, that stocks were overvalued and bonds were undervalued based on the presence of mean reversion, they would sell stocks and buy bonds until these assets reached their fair values. Thus, the notion of mean reversion is a catch-22. If mean reversion exists, investors would exploit it so that misvalued assets would be corrected instantaneously. Therefore, it cannot exist (unless, of course, investors differ in their opinion of fair value).[4]

Despite the philosophical arguments against mean reversion and, by extension, the wisdom of tactical asset allocation, the evidence is ambiguous. Although most studies historically have failed to reject the hypothesis that most asset prices follow a random walk,[5] more recent studies suggest the presence of negative serial correlation in stock and bond returns over long time periods, which, of course, is precisely what we would expect to observe from a mean reverting process.[6]

IMPLEMENTATION

Suppose we accept the view that from time to time an asset's price departs from its equilibrium or fair value. How do we implement a tactical asset allocation strategy? There are a variety of approaches for exploiting deviations from fair value. We will describe one representative approach merely to illustrate how we can exploit the notion of mean reversion.

Suppose we wish to allocate a fund between stocks and bonds. First, we must estimate the expected return of each asset class. If we believe in mean reversion, expected return equals the income we expect to receive plus the change in price we expect will occur when the asset moves from its current price to its fair value, all divided by current price. Even if an asset is fairly valued, its price should change as the growth rate of its income stream changes. Therefore, for stocks, we can estimate return as shown in Formula 3–1.[7]

Formula 3–1   Expected Return for Stocks

$$R = \frac{\overbrace{E \cdot (1+g) \cdot p}^{\text{INCOME}} + \overbrace{E \cdot (1+g) \cdot PE - P}^{\text{APPRECIATION}}}{P}$$

where

   R = Expected return for stocks
   E = Last period's earnings
   g = Growth rate of earnings
   p = Dividend payout ratio
   PE = Equilibrium price/earnings multiple
   P = Current stock price

We can easily rearrange Formula 3–1 to make it more concise, but in its current format we can readily see that return equals the income we receive ($E \cdot (1 + g) \cdot p$) plus the change in price ($E \cdot (1 + g) \cdot PE - P$), all divided by our starting price.

We can express the expected return for bonds in similar fashion, as shown in Formula 3–2:[8]

Formula 3–2 Expected Return for Bonds

$$R = \frac{C + C/i + (F - C/i) / (1+i)^n - P}{P}$$

where

   R = Expected return for bonds
   C = Coupon payment
   i = Equilibrium yield to maturity
   F = Face value
   P = Current bond price
   n = Term to maturity at end of investment horizon

Formulae 3–1 and 3–2 enable us to estimate the expected returns for stocks and bonds, respectively. In general, if we expect stocks to produce a higher return than bonds, we allocate more of our fund to stocks, while we would allocate more to bonds if we believed bonds would generate a higher return. There are many ways to determine how aggressively we should act on our convictions. For example, in order to maximize the fund's expected return, we would allocate the entire fund to the asset class with the higher expected return. However, such concentration greatly increases the risk that, over any particular investment horizon, we could experience extremely poor performance. As an alternative to concentrating the fund in one asset class or the other, we can scale the fund's exposure according to some heuristic. For example, we can estimate the variability of the spreads in stock and bond returns and allocate the fund in accordance with the probability that one asset class will outperform the other. The standard deviation of the spread in stock and bond returns is computed as shown in Formula 3–3.

Formula 3–3 Standard Deviation of Spread in Stock and Bond Returns

$$S = \sqrt{S_S^2 + S_B^2 - 2 \cdot r \cdot S_S \cdot S_B}$$

where

S = Standard deviation of spread between stock and bond returns

S_S = Standard deviation of stock returns

S_B = Standard deviation of bond returns

r = Correlation between stock and bond returns

By dividing the expected spread in stock and bond returns by the standard deviation of the spreads, we can estimate the significance of the spread and thus the probability that stocks will outperform bonds or vice versa (see Chapter 1). If we estimate that there is a 75 percent chance that stocks will outperform bonds, a reasonable heuristic might be to allocate 75 percent of our fund to stocks and 25 percent to bonds.

Let us demonstrate this process with an example. Suppose we assume the following values for stocks:

Stock price	$100
Last period's earnings	$ 8
Dividend payout ratio	40%
Growth in earnings	10%
Equilibrium price/earnings multiple	12

By substituting these values into Formula 3–1, we can estimate the expected return for stocks as:

$$R = \frac{8 \cdot (1.1) \cdot .4 + 8 \cdot (1.1) \cdot 12 - 100}{100} = .0912$$

Thus, based on the dividend income we expect to receive and the change in price that we expect to occur as stocks revert to their equilibrium value, we expect stocks to return 9.12 percent.

Now let us estimate the expected return for bonds, based on the following assumptions:

Bond price	$100
Coupon	$ 9
Face value	$100
Equilibrium yield to maturity	9.5%
Term to maturity	15

$$R = \frac{9 + 9/.095 + (100 - 9/.095)/(1.095)^{15} - 100}{100} = .0521$$

Given our expectation for coupon income and price change should bonds move from their current price to their equilibrium value, we expect bonds to return 5.21 percent. Thus we expect stocks to return 3.91 percent more than bonds (9.12% − 5.21%).

Our next task is to determine the significance of a 3.91 percent spread between the expected return of stocks and that of bonds. Suppose that stocks have a standard deviation of 20 percent while bonds have a standard deviation of 10 percent. Further suppose that stocks and bonds are 30 percent correlated with each other. We can estimate the standard deviation of the spread in their returns as:

$$S = \sqrt{.2^2 + .1^2 - 2 \cdot .3 \cdot .2 \cdot .1} = .1949$$

If we assume that the spread in stock and bond returns is normally distributed, we simply divide the expected spread of 3.91 percent by the standard deviation of the spread (19.49%), and look this value up in a normal distribution table. By following this procedure, we find that the probability of stocks outperforming bonds equals 58 percent. Thus, based on the heuristic described earlier, we would allocate 58 percent of our fund to stocks and 42 percent to bonds. If the standard deviation of the spread were only 3 percent, a 3.91 percent spread would be much more significant, and we would be more confident (specifically, 90 percent) that stocks would outperform bonds. If, on the other hand, the standard deviation were 30 percent, our confidence that stocks would outperform bonds would only equal 55 percent.

Suppose that we proceed according to this heuristic and stocks suddenly increase 10 percent so that our stock price now equals $110. Suppose we still believe that our earlier assumptions about earnings growth, the payout ratio, and the equilibrium values for the price/earnings multiple and yield to maturity are appropriate. The only change is that stock prices are now 10 percent higher. If we again substitute the appropriate values into Formula 3–1 to compute the expected return for stocks, we find that it has fallen to −0.80 percent.

$$R = \frac{8 \cdot (1.1)\ .4 + 8 \cdot (1.1) \cdot 12 - 110}{110} = -.008$$

Thus the spread between the expected return for stocks and the expected return for bonds changes to −6.01 percent, and the probability that stocks will outperform bonds falls to 38 percent.

$$-6.01\%/19.49\% = -.3084 \text{ (implies 38\%)}$$

Now suppose stocks decline to $95 and again none of our other assumptions change, including our expectations about bonds. Our expected return for stocks increases to 14.86 percent.

$$R = \frac{8 \cdot (1.1) \cdot .4 + 8 \cdot (1.1) \cdot 12 - 95}{95} = .1486$$

With an expected return of 14.86 percent for stocks, the spread between stocks and bonds increases to 9.65 percent, and the probability that stocks will outperform bonds increases to 69 percent.

It should be intuitively pleasing that our allocation to stocks increases as stock prices fall and decreases as stock prices rise, as long as our other assumptions remain unchanged. The logic is quite straightforward. As stock prices rise, the opportunity for further gains diminishes. By the same logic, as stock prices fall, the opportunity for gains increases as long as stock prices are anchored to an equilibrium value. In Figure 3–1, we show the relationship among the price of stocks, the expected return of stocks, and the allocation to stocks assuming that all other variables remain constant.

In these examples, we have focused on only one variable—the price of stocks. In practice, several of the variables may change simultaneously. In all likelihood, an increase in the price of stocks will accompany an

FIGURE 3–1
Price, Expected Return, and Allocation

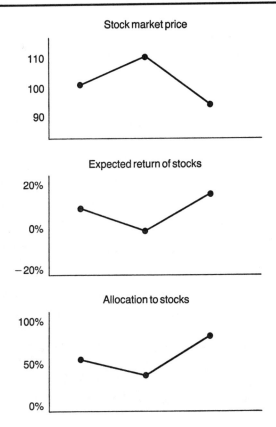

increase in earnings or the growth rate of earnings. In this case the equilibrium value of stocks would also rise so that the expected return may not change at all. In many instances, though, stock and bond prices change in response to a change in investor sentiment without any accompanying change in the underlying fundamentals. It is instances such as these that create opportunity for tactical asset allocators.

Performance

The tactical asset allocation strategy we have described requires that we forecast several variables: the growth rate of earnings, the dividend payout ratio, the equilibrium price/earnings multiple, and the equilibrium yield to maturity. How dependent is the success of the strategy on our ability to forecast these variables accurately? If asset values do indeed fluctuate within a relatively narrow interval around equilibrium relationships, it is possible to add value with virtually no forecasting ability. The discipline of tactical asset allocation by itself will generate profits. For example, suppose we are completely naive about forecasting the required inputs for our model and use the following default assumptions:

Earnings:	Annual earnings as of previous month
Payout ratio:	Payout ratio as of previous month
Growth rate:	Annual growth rate over previous four years
Equilibrium P/E:	Historical relationship of P/E multiple to Aa (double A credit rating) corporate interest rates from January 1958 to December 1977 applied to previous month's Aa corporate interest rate
Equilibrium yield to maturity:	Previous month's Aa corporate interest rate

If we had applied our simple tactical asset allocation strategy to stocks and bonds beginning in January 1978 and ending in December 1987, rebalancing each month between the Standard & Poor's 500 Stock Average and long-term corporate bonds, we would have achieved a total return of 17.92 percent per year before transaction costs. If, instead, we allocated 50 percent of our fund to stocks and 50 percent to bonds at the beginning of the period and left it alone for the next 10 years, we would have

FIGURE 3–2
Cumulative Wealth—Tactical Asset Allocation versus Buy-and-Hold

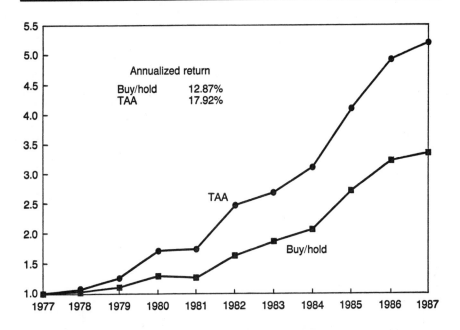

achieved an annual return of 12.87 percent. Hence, we could have added more than 5 percent per year to a buy-and-hold strategy merely by following a disciplined rule with naive inputs. Figure 3–2 contrasts the cumulative wealth generated by our simple tactical asset allocation strategy with earnings of a buy-and-hold strategy that starts out equally divided between stocks and bonds.

Not only did this strategy improve performance by more than 5 percent per year, but it added value in 9 out of 10 years from 1978 through 1987. The year-by-year results of the tactical asset allocation strategy and a buy-and-hold strategy are shown in Table 3–1.

As impressive as these results may seem, they should be taken with a very large grain of salt. Performance results for tactical asset allocation

TABLE 3–1
Year-by-Year Results

Period	Stocks	Bonds	Tactical Asset Allocation	Buy-and-Hold	Value Added
1978	6.56%	−0.07%	6.57%	3.24%	3.33%
1979	18.44%	−4.18%	18.44%	7.49%	10.95%
1980	32.42%	−2.62%	36.39%	17.31%	19.08%
1981	−4.91%	−0.96%	0.95%	−3.50%	4.45%
1982	21.41%	43.79%	43.16%	29.63%	13.53%
1983	22.51%	4.70%	8.35%	15.25%	−6.90%
1984	6.27%	16.39%	15.56%	10.02%	5.54%
1985	32.16%	30.90%	32.57%	31.67%	0.90%
1986	18.77%	18.63%	19.82%	18.72%	1.10%
1987	5.25%	1.84%	5.15%	1.84%	3.31%
1978–87	15.29%	9.85%	17.93%	12.87%	5.06%

strategies can be extremely *period specific.*

SUMMARY

- Tactical asset allocation is based on the presumption of mean reversion. Specifically, it presumes that asset class prices fluctuate around equilibrium values.
- Tactical asset allocation is typically executed by shifting a fund to the asset class with the higher near-term expected return. Typically, the near-term expected return of an asset class changes inversely with changes in the price of the asset class.
- Most disciplined approaches to tactical asset allocation add value with minimal forecasting skill as long as asset class prices follow a mean reverting process.
- Investment results from tactical asset allocation strategies may be period specific; hence, we are well advised to view them with caution.

NOTES

1. The term *tactical asset allocation* encompasses a wide variety of approaches for varying a portfolio's asset mix. Some of these approaches may be driven

by momentum models rather than mean reversion models or they may combine elements of both models. Also, some tactical asset allocators may attempt to gauge investor sentiment or they may rely on economic and political indicators. The point is that tactical asset allocation based upon the principle of mean reversion is not the only approach. It is, however, a crucial underpinning of most of the valuation-driven approaches, which, in some instances, is unknown to the user.

2. For example, see R. Merton, "A Simple Model of Capital Market Equilibrium with Incomplete Information," *Journal of Finance* (July 1987), pp. 483–510.

3. For example, see R. Shiller, "Do Stock Prices Move Too Much to Be Justified by Subsequent Changes in Dividends?" *American Economic Review* (June 1981), pp. 421–436.

4. Also, mean reversion may exist to the extent that investors have heterogeneous expectations about the speed with which asset prices return to their equilibrium values.

5. For example, see E. Fama, "Efficient Capital Markets: A Review of Theory and Empirical Work," *Journal of Finance* 25, pp. 383–417.

6. For example, see E. Fama and K. French, "Dividend Yields and Expected Stock Returns," *Journal of Financial Economics* (October 1988), pp. 3–25; also see J. Poterba and L. Summers, "Mean Reversion in Stock Prices: Evidence and Implications," *Journal of Financial Economics* (October 1988), pp. 27–59.

7. This formula assumes that income is received only at the end of the investment horizon. If we wished to incorporate interim cash flows, we would simply find the internal rate of return that discounted all of the cash flows (including terminal price) back to the stock's current price.

8. Again, this formula assumes that income is received only at the end of the investment horizon. If we wished to incorporate interim cash flows, we would proceed as described in footnote 7.

CHAPTER 4

SIMPLIFYING ASSET ALLOCATION WITH LINEAR INVESTMENT RULES

"Americans have a compulsion for digging deeper and deeper into the surface of things."

Oscar Wilde

INTRODUCTION

In the previous three chapters we presented the principal approaches to asset allocation. Even though we abstracted from much of the underlying theoretical detail and instead concentrated on the mathematics required to implement the strategies, parts of our discussion may have seemed to lend support to Oscar Wilde's observation. In this chapter, we attempt to cut through the surface. We demonstrate how we can capture the essence of complex dynamic strategies with simple linear investment rules. We hasten to add that these rules are approximations of the strategies they are intended to replicate. Nonetheless, these rules help us to understand the essence of dynamic strategies and the conditions which are favorable or unfavorable to the success of dynamic strategies. Most of the insights that we discuss in this chapter were introduced by André Perold and William Sharpe in a 1988 paper entitled "Dynamic Strategies for Asset Allocation."[1]

PAYOFF FUNCTIONS FOR BUY-AND-HOLD STRATEGIES

Suppose we have a choice of allocating a fund between two risky assets which we call asset A and asset B. Suppose that each asset is currently valued at $100. Let us define their relative value as the ratio of asset A to asset B. Thus their relative value currently equals 1.00. Now let us define a graph where the horizontal axis represents the relative value of asset A to asset B and the vertical axis represents incremental return relative to asset B. Now consider a strategy whereby we allocate 100 percent of our fund to asset A. How do we represent this strategy on our graph? This strategy's incremental return has a one-to-one correspondence to the relative value of asset A to asset B; hence we represent it as a straight line starting at the origin and proceeding at a 45 degree angle as shown in Figure 4–1. This graph is called a *payoff diagram* and the line representing the relationship between the relative value of asset A to asset B and the incremental return associated with a 100 percent allocation to asset A is called a *payoff function.*

Now imagine a strategy whereby we allocate our fund entirely to asset B. What does this strategy's payoff function look like? It would be a straight horizontal line located at 0 percent incremental return, since asset

FIGURE 4–1
100% Allocation to Asset A

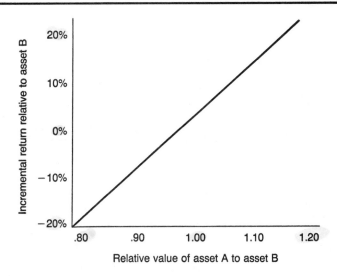

B's incremental return relative to itself is obviously 0 percent (see Figure 4–2).

Now suppose we allocate 50 percent of our fund to asset A and 50 percent to asset B. What does the payoff function of this strategy look like? It is a straight line exactly halfway between the payoff function representing a 100 percent allocation to asset A and the payoff function representing a 100 percent allocation to asset B, as depicted in Figure 4–3.

The three strategies we have just described assume that we do not alter our initial allocation even to restore the fund's initial mix. Thus, in our example, where we started with a 50 percent allocation to each asset, the actual exposure changes with the relative performance of two assets. We refer to such strategies as *buy-and-hold strategies*. Buy-and-hold strategies always have straight line payoff functions. In our discussion of strategic asset allocation in Chapter 1, we assumed implicitly that we bought and held the efficient asset mixes. In fact, the probabilistic statements that we made about the various asset mixes depended on the assumption that we did not alter the asset mixes after our initial allocation.

FIGURE 4–2
100% Allocation to Asset B

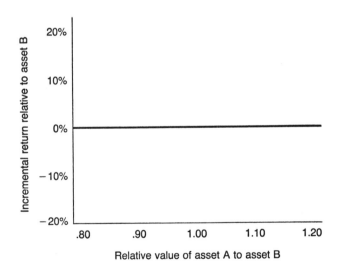

FIGURE 4–3
Equal Allocation to Asset A and Asset B

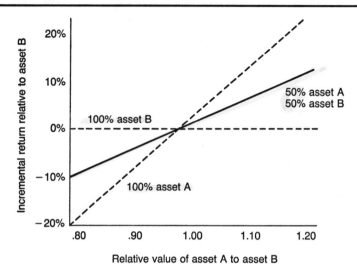

Relative value of asset A to asset B

PAYOFF FUNCTIONS FOR DYNAMIC STRATEGIES

Now suppose we follow a strategy whereby we change a fund's exposure based on the relative performance of the component assets. For example, what would a payoff function look like for a strategy whereby we increased a fund's exposure to an asset as the asset's relative value increased and decreased the fund's exposure to that asset as its relative value decreased? The payoff function for this strategy is *convex,* as shown in Figure 4–4.

What if, instead of favoring the asset with the better relative performance, we increased a fund's exposure to an asset as its relative value declined and decreased the exposure to this asset as its relative value increased? The payoff function for this type of strategy is *concave,* as depicted in Figure 4–5.

FIGURE 4–4
Convex Strategy

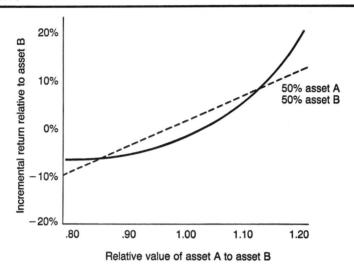

FIGURE 4–5
Concave Strategy

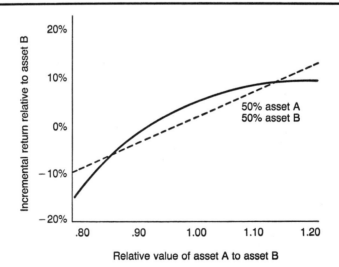

SIMPLE LINEAR INVESTMENT RULES FOR DYNAMIC STRATEGIES

Suppose we wish to pursue a strategy that generates a convex payoff function. We could achieve this result by multiplying the change in an asset's percentage allocation caused by that asset's relative performance by some factor greater than 1 and adding this value to the asset's percentage allocation before the return-induced change. For example, suppose we start out with a $100 fund allocated equally to asset A and asset B, and suppose we choose 5 for our factor to induce convexity in the payoff function. In Table 4–1, we show how our fund's allocation would change according to this simple linear investment rule if asset A returned 5 percent and asset B returned 0 percent.

In order to induce a concave payoff function, we could follow the same investment rule used to generate a convex payoff function, but instead of a factor equal to 5, we must choose a factor that is less than 1. Suppose, for example, that we choose a factor equal to –5. We show these results in Table 4–2.

If we choose a factor equal to 0 for our linear investment rule, we would exactly restore the previous mix, while a factor equal to 1 would generate the same outcome as a buy-and-hold strategy. The magnitude of the factor affects how aggressively we pursue a convex or concave strategy. The larger the absolute value of the factor, the more aggressive is our approach to the strategy.

TABLE 4–1
A Linear Investment Rule to Produce a Convex Payoff Function

Factor = 5
Asset A return = 5%
Asset B return = 0%

	Initial Value	Initial Percent	Return	New Value	New Percent	Revised Percent	Revised Value
Asset A	50.00	50.00%	5.00%	52.50	51.22%	56.10%	57.50
Asset B	50.00	50.00%	0.00%	50.00	48.78%	43.90%	45.00
Total	100.00	100.00%		102.50	100.00%	100.00%	102.50

TABLE 4–2
A Linear Investment Rule to Produce a Concave Payoff Function

Factor = −5
Asset A return = 5%
Asset B return = 0%

	Initial Value	Initial Percent	Return	New Value	New Percent	Revised Percent	Revised Value
Asset A	50.00	50.00%	5.00%	52.50	51.22%	43.90%	45.00
Asset B	50.00	50.00%	0.00%	50.00	48.78%	56.10%	57.50
Total	100.00	100.00%		102.50	100.00	100.00%	102.50

CONDITIONS FAVORABLE TO CONVEX AND CONCAVE STRATEGIES

When is it preferable to generate a strategy with a convex payoff function? We can answer this question simply by examining a convex payoff function. When the value of the assets between which we are allocating our fund diverge significantly, a strategy with a convex payoff function will add value to a buy-and-hold strategy. On the other hand, if the value of the assets between which we are allocating our fund do not diverge very much, but instead vibrate within a narrow interval, a strategy with a concave payoff function will add value to a buy-and-hold strategy. These comparisons are shown in Figure 4–6.

We can determine whether asset values tend to diverge or vibrate within a narrow interval by examining the serial correlation of their net returns (the difference in their returns). If their net returns are positively serially correlated (last period's net return is positively associated with this period's net return), then their net returns tend to follow trends leading to divergent values. If, instead, the net returns of the assets are negatively serially correlated (last period's net return is inversely associated with this period's net return), then their net returns follow a mean reverting process (frequent reversals), and the assets' values are not likely to diverge very much.

In Table 4–3, we demonstrate this principle by computing the cumulative wealth of a buy-and-hold strategy, a convex strategy, and a concave

FIGURE 4–6

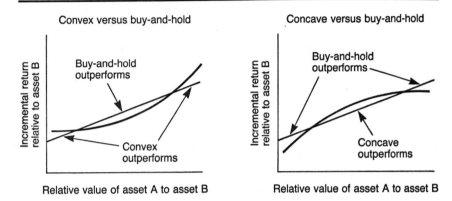

strategy, assuming the net returns of the assets are 100 percent positively serially correlated.[2]

Next, in Table 4–4, we contrive a pattern of reversals in net return (–100 percent serially correlated) and show the cumulative wealth of a buy-and-hold strategy, a convex strategy, and a concave strategy.

CORRESPONDENCE TO DYNAMIC HEDGING STRATEGIES AND TACTICAL ASSET ALLOCATION

It should be apparent that there is a direct correspondence between the simple rules we described to induce convexity and concavity and the more complex strategies for dynamic hedging and tactical asset allocation. Dynamic hedging strategies require us to shift a fund toward a risky asset as the portfolio rises in value and away from the risky asset as the portfolio falls in value. The rules governing the precise magnitude of the shift in allocation, especially for traditional portfolio insurance, are quite complex. Nonetheless, the essence of both our simple convex strategy and portfolio insurance is to "buy high and sell low." In fact, if we recall the payoff function of a portfolio insurance strategy, we notice that it too is convex, although it has a kink in it. The payoff function for constant proportion

TABLE 4–3
Positively Serially Correlated Net Returns

		Cumulative Wealth		
Asset 1	Asset 2	Buy-and-Hold	Convex	Concave
50.00	50.00	100.00	100.00	100.00
52.50	50.00	102.50	102.50	102.50
55.13	50.00	105.13	105.38	104.75
57.88	50.00	107.88	108.66	106.73
60.78	50.00	110.78	112.33	108.45
63.81	50.00	113.81	116.43	109.90
67.00	50.00	117.00	120.96	111.10
70.36	50.00	120.36	125.92	112.08
73.87	50.00	123.87	131.31	112.87
77.57	50.00	127.57	137.12	113.50
81.44	50.00	131.44	143.35	113.99

portfolio insurance, however, looks exactly like the convex curves for our simple linear investment rule. Thus, portfolio insurance will tend to add value to a buy-and-hold alternative when the risky asset value departs significantly from the riskless asset value. This concept is analogous to investment in options. If the assumed variability that underlies the price of an option on a risky asset systematically understates the experienced variability of that asset (and thus the tendency for its value to change substantially), investment in the option should be a profitable strategy over the long run.

Now let us consider tactical asset allocation. Unlike portfolio insurance, we must forecast asset class returns, so how can we replicate tactical asset allocation with reactive linear investment rules? Although ostensibly we forecast asset class returns, in many, if not most, applications of tactical asset allocation the most variable component of our forecast model is current price. For example, in Chapter 3, we based our forecast of stock return on current price, last year's earnings, the dividend payout ratio, growth in earnings, and the equilibrium price/earnings multiple. Of all these inputs, current price is the most variable. The same is true in the case of bonds. Price is more variable than coupons, term to maturity, and the equilibrium yield to maturity. It is possible, of course, that we can aggressively change our estimate of the equilibrium price/earnings

TABLE 4–4
Negatively Serially Correlated Net Returns

		Cumulative Wealth		
Asset 1	Asset 2	Buy-and-Hold	Convex	Concave
50.00	50.00	100.00	100.00	100.00
52.50	50.00	102.50	102.50	102.50
49.88	50.00	99.88	99.63	100.25
52.37	50.00	102.37	102.10	102.77
49.75	50.00	99.75	99.25	100.50
52.24	50.00	102.24	101.71	103.03
49.63	50.00	99.63	98.88	100.75
52.11	50.00	102.11	101.32	103.30
49.50	50.00	99.50	98.51	101.00
51.98	50.00	101.98	100.93	103.57
49.38	50.00	99.38	98.15	101.25

multiple or yield to maturity, but it is not likely that the actual, albeit unobservable values, change very much over short time periods. Thus, if changes in our forecast of asset returns reflect mostly changes in the current prices of the respective assets, we can capture the essence of tactical asset allocation with a simple investment rule such as the one we described earlier to induce a concave payoff function. This correspondence should be apparent if we recall the relationship between the price of stocks and exposure to stocks in our example of tactical asset allocation in Chapter 3. At a price of $100, we allocated 58 percent of our fund to stocks. When we assumed that all of the inputs to our forecast models remained unchanged except stock price (which rose to $110), we lowered our stock exposure to 35 percent. When we assumed a fall in stock price to $95, our stock exposure increased to 85 percent.

If instead of performing the calculations required by our tactical asset allocation strategy, we merely followed our simple linear investment rule to generate a concave payoff function using a factor of −10 and starting with the same initial allocation, our corresponding allocations to stocks would have been 37 percent when the stock price increased to $110 and 68 percent when the stock price decreased to $95. This compares rather closely to the allocations that resulted from our more complex approach, as we show in Table 4–5.

TABLE 4–5
Correspondence between Tactical Asset Allocation and a Concave Strategy

Stock Price	Percent Allocated to Stocks	
	Valuation-Based Forecast Model	Concave Linear Investment Rule
$100	58%	58%
$110	38%	37%
$ 95	69%	68%

We do not claim that simple linear investment rules capture all of the subtleties of more complex dynamic strategies such as portfolio insurance and various approaches to tactical asset allocation and thus should serve as a substitute for these strategies. Rather, we merely wish to convey the essence of these more complex strategies by focusing on simpler rules. In so doing, we hope to draw attention to the implicit forecasts of portfolio insurers and tactical asset allocators who pursue these and similar strategies to enhance a fund's return. Those who follow portfolio insurance strategies or, more generally, strategies with convex payoff functions, believe implicitly that the asset classes between which they allocate their funds will experience divergent holding period returns. Conversely, investors who pursue valuation-based tactical asset allocation strategies implicitly believe that the asset classes between which they allocate their fund will experience similar holding period returns and that their relative values will vibrate within a narrow interval.[3]

SUMMARY

- The essence of dynamic strategies such as portfolio insurance and tactical asset allocation can be captured with simple linear investment rules.
- Dynamic strategies that require us to buy an asset as its relative value rises and to sell an asset as its relative value falls generate convex payoff functions.
- Dynamic strategies that require us to sell an asset as its relative

value rises and to buy an asset as its relative value falls generate concave payoff functions.

- Strategies with convex payoff functions add value when the net returns of the assets between which the fund is allocated are positively serially correlated (trends) leading to divergent holding period values.
- Strategies with concave payoff functions add value when the net returns of the assets between which the fund is allocated are negatively serially correlated (reversals) leading to similar holding period returns.

NOTES

1. A. Perold and W. Sharpe, "Dynamic Strategies for Asset Allocation," *Financial Analysts Journal* (January/February 1988), pp. 16–27.
2. In this example, we induced convexity in the payoff function as follows: we started with an equal allocation to each asset. Then we multiplied the change in the exposure to each asset that was caused by their relative performance by a factor equal to 5. We added this change to the previous percentage exposure for each asset and rebalanced the portfolio to accord with this new percentage exposure. We induced concavity in the payoff function by following the same rule with the exception that we used a factor equal to −5.
3. Throughout our discussion, we have assumed implicitly that we shift a fund between two assets. All of the arguments we have made apply equally to a situation in which we allocate a fund among several assets.

AMERICAN FABRIC: PART 1

We now leave behind theory and formulae and reenter the real world (the fictional real world, that is). We join Betsy Ross, a newly minted MBA, as she embarks upon her career at American Fabric. The names and events are fictional. Any resemblance to real people, living, deceased, or yet to arrive, is purely coincidental.

On June 14, 1987, Betsy Ross joined the Treasurer's staff of American Fabric, having graduated the previous month from New York University with an MBA in finance. During her interview, Betsy expressed interest in applying some of the quantitative concepts she had studied in her courses, especially those dealing with portfolio theory. She was intrigued, she had told her interviewer, with the compelling logic and rigor of portfolio theory. In fact, she had written her master's thesis on the application of portfolio theory to asset allocation. She was somewhat surprised, although undaunted, to learn that American Fabric approached investment decisions more traditionally and had yet to incorporate quantitative methods into their investment process.

Betsy was assigned to work for Patrick Henry, who was the Assistant Treasurer of American Fabric. Among Patrick's responsibilities was the investment management of American Fabric's pension fund. In this capacity he reported to an Investment Committee comprised of several of American Fabric's senior officers. Patrick was impressed by Betsy's strength of conviction regarding investment management, not to mention her 3.9 grade point average. (She had received a C in her technical analysis course, which she attributed to philosophical differences with her instructor.) Patrick hoped that Betsy's quantitative bent would bring a refreshing perspective to the Investment Committee at American Fabric, which had a collective disdain for quantitative methods or any methods introduced since their graduation from college. They relied strictly on "good, old-fashioned judgment and experience" to determine the investment posture of American Fabric's pension fund.

As of March 31, 1988, American Fabric's pension fund totaled $120 million, of which 70 percent was invested in government bonds and 30 percent in short-term securities. Nine months earlier, the pension fund had been valued at $145 million, 80 percent of which was invested in stocks with the balance invested in junk bonds. Needless to say, the stock market crash went a long way toward reducing the fund's stock exposure. Panic selling on the part of the Investment Committee completed the reallocation to fixed-income investments.

Tom Paine, President of American Fabric, had met Betsy at a cocktail reception for new MBAs. Although he found her to be intelligent and articulate, he did not have much interest in the pension fund department where Betsy was assigned—until the fund lost $25 million in the crash. Although Paine did not understand all the details of the new pension accounting rules, he believed that a further substantial decline in pension fund assets could impair American Fabric's balance sheet and reduce its income as well. He decided it was time to get involved in the investment management of the pension fund; he would attend next month's Investment Committee meeting.

Since joining American Fabric, Betsy had attended all of the Investment Committee meetings, where she was responsible for taking the minutes. She obviously was quite surprised when Paine entered the conference room as July's meeting got underway. Paine expressed his concern about the sharp decline in the pension fund assets and the impact a further decline might have on American Fabric's ability to raise capital. He also questioned the Investment Committee's decision to retreat from the stock market at a time when stocks were valued 15 percent below their previous year's peak. He wondered aloud whether or not the Committee had substituted fear and greed for objectivity and logic.

As various members of the Committee responded to Paine, first in turn and then simultaneously competing for his attention, he realized that indeed they had become slaves to their emotions. The situation beckoned for a drastic response, and Paine hadn't ascended to the presidency by shying away from such challenges.

After restoring order among the Committee members, he asked Patrick to prepare an asset allocation study for his direct review and he suggested that Patrick assign this project to Betsy since he was aware of her expertise in asset allocation. Moreover, he directed the Committee to provide Betsy with its best estimates of return for stocks, bonds, and short-term securities covering the next five years, together with a range of returns which they believed would encompass two thirds of the probable outcomes for each of the asset classes.

Betsy was somewhat nervous about her assignment, but more than that, she was excited and eager. Betsy expressed her appreciation to Paine for his confidence in her. Patrick was pleased with Paine's decision and especially his suggestion to involve Betsy in the project. He was more than willing to delegate the assignment to Betsy since he believed that she had a much deeper understanding of asset allocation than he did.

When Betsy received the return estimates from the Investment Committee, she was initially frustrated by the qualifications surrounding each of the estimates, but eventually she was able to translate the Committee's circumspection into specific values for expected return and risk. Based on its forecasts and the surrounding high and low estimates, Betsy was able to infer the expected return and standard deviation for stocks, bonds, and short-term securities.

	Expected Return	Standard Deviation
Stocks	13.0%	21.0%
Bonds	9.5%	10.0%
Short-term securities	7.0%	2.0%

Betsy realized that the only additional information she needed to identify the portfolios that formed the efficient frontier was the correlations between each pair of asset classes. She decided that a reasonable point of departure for estimating these values would be the historical relationships of the asset classes. She gathered the historical monthly returns of the Standard & Poor's 500 Stock Average, long-term corporate bonds, and 90-day Treasury bills for the last 30 years and entered the data into a computer spreadsheet. She performed regressions between stocks and bonds, stocks and Treasury bills, and bonds and Treasury bills. She computed the square root of the coefficients of determination and changed their sign when necessary to agree with the sign of the regression coefficient.

Betsy computed these correlations over three separate periods.

	Stocks & Bonds	Stocks & Bills	Bonds & Bills
1958–67	21.4%	−16.0%	1.3%
1968–77	46.4%	−23.0%	3.9%
1978–87	32.2%	−14.6%	5.7%

As she expected, stocks and bonds were the most highly correlated, since they are both long-term assets. She was comfortable with the inverse correlation between stocks and Treasury bills, since a rise in interest rates would lower the present value of future dividend payments while raising the income from short-term investments. The fact that bonds and Treasury bills were slightly positively correlated, Betsy reasoned, was due to the offsetting effect interest rate changes have on reinvestment income and valuation.

Since the results were relatively stable across the three measurement periods, and since she believed that the most recent past best characterized the Committee's expectations for the foreseeable future, Betsy used the following correlations in her analysis:

Stocks and bonds	30.0%
Stocks and Treasury bills	−15.0%
Bonds and Treasury bills	5.0%

Now she had all the necessary information to identify the efficient portfolios. She simply needed to find the asset weights that minimized risk for each level of expected return. Betsy was aware that most large-scale optimization problems require linear or quadratic programs, but she did not have access to such software, and Paine's reputation for frugality was legendary. Because she was dealing with only three asset classes, she decided to solve for the asset weights of the efficient portfolios herself by employing the matrix inversion routine included in her spreadsheet software. On her first attempt, she noticed that several of the efficient portfolios had negative weights. She knew that short selling was unacceptable so she reoptimized the portfolios that had negative weights by excluding the asset class that would have been sold short.[1] It took her less than 10 minutes to arrive at the minimum risk portfolio for each level of expected return she had specified.

Betsy observed that a 100 percent position in the least risky asset, short-term securities, would not be a desirable choice, since she could increase expected return and reduce risk by diversifying into stocks and bonds. By iteratively raising the expected return by small increments above 7 percent and solving for the minimum risk portfolio, she discovered that the minimum risk "efficient" portfolio had an expected return of 7.2 percent and a standard deviation of 1.9 percent. She prepared a table for Paine showing a range of efficient asset mixes, along with their expected returns and standard deviations. After reviewing the results with Patrick, the two of them met with Paine.

	1	2	3	4	5	6	7
Stock (percent)	2.4	10.3	20.2	30.1	42.9	71.4	100.0
Bond (percent)	2.2	15.2	31.5	47.8	57.1	28.6	0.0
Short-term (percent)	95.4	74.5	48.3	22.1	0.0	0.0	0.0
Expected return (percent)	7.2	8.0	9.0	10.0	11.0	12.0	13.0
Standard deviation (percent)	1.9	3.2	6.0	9.0	12.0	16.1	21.0

Paine studied the results as Betsy interpreted them. She explained that these portfolios were the least risky, given their respective expected returns, and that she could easily identify other efficient portfolios if he were to specify an expected return that was not included in her analysis.

Paine responded, "These results are very interesting, but how do I know which portfolio is most suitable for our pension fund?"

Betsy wasn't quite sure how to phrase her answer, so she decided to give it to him straight and hope for the best. "Well, sir," she said, "I need to know more about your utility curve." From the quizzical expression on Paine's face, she knew immediately that this approach was the wrong one, but it was too late.

"My what?" Paine said.

"In order for me to recommend a specific asset mix, I need to understand more about your attitude toward risk. For example, sir, portfolio 1 has an expected return of 7.2 percent and a standard deviation of 1.9 percent. Would you be willing to incur more risk to raise the fund's expected return?"

"Well, yes, I suppose," responded Paine.

"Would you be comfortable with portfolio 7?" asked Betsy.

"I don't think it would be prudent to invest the entire fund in the stock market," said Paine. "What if it crashes again?"

"That's my point," explained Betsy. "In order to identify the optimal asset mix, we need to identify those combinations of expected return and standard deviation between which you are indifferent. That's your utility curve. Once we have that information, we can find the asset mix that is tangent to your utility curve."

Betsy could see that she wasn't making much progress; in fact, it seemed as though Paine was beginning to lose patience with her. After a short period of awkward silence, he finally looked at her and said, "How would you describe your utility curve?"

"It's definitely quadratic," she said, "but I'm not sure how I would quantify my risk aversion."

As she thought about his question and her response, she realized that he was perfectly justified in his confusion. Utility theory is fine in the classroom, but it doesn't translate very well in the CEO's office.

"Betsy," asked Patrick who had remained silent up until now, "isn't there some other approach we can use to find out which of these asset mixes to adopt?"

"Actually, Patrick, I have an idea. What if I were to estimate the likelihood that each of these asset mixes has of achieving some level of return which we consider important? We could find all of the asset mixes that provide sufficient confidence of achieving this critical return and select the mix with the highest expected return from that group."

"Now you're talking," said Paine. "If the fund loses another 5 percent, American Fabric will show a pension liability on its balance sheet. We cannot permit that to happen."

"Then the critical return is −5 percent," Betsy said.

"Yes, I want to be extremely confident that we won't lose more than 5 percent. Can you find an asset mix that will achieve my objective, Betsy?"

"I can show you results by tomorrow, sir. What time would be convenient for you?"

Paine looked at his schedule and asked her to meet with him at 3:30 the next day.

Betsy felt relieved as she returned to her office. What began as an embarrassment seemed to be proceeding more smoothly. She decided to stay late and complete the analysis that night. First, she went to her bookcase and retrieved her statistics book. She quickly flipped to the back and found the normal distribution table. Then she took the results she had prepared for Paine. She subtracted each asset mix's expected return from −5 percent, the return that Paine deemed critical, and divided this result by the standard deviation of each mix to standardize the spread between the expected return and the critical return. Then she looked up these values in the normal distribution table to estimate the likelihood that each mix would achieve the critical return. She also repeated the analysis, but this time she divided each asset mix's standard deviation by the square root of 5 to determine the probability each mix had of achieving the critical return on average over a five-year horizon. Then, she raised the single year probability estimates to the fifth power to determine the chance of meeting Paine's objective each and every year within the five-year horizon. Finally, she was ready to meet with Paine. Since Patrick would be out of town, Betsy would have to meet with Paine by herself, but she was not concerned.

The next day Betsy double-checked her results from beginning to end. She arrived at Paine's office five minutes early. Paine was on the phone when his secretary informed him of Betsy's arrival. After a few minutes, he came out to the reception area and asked her into his office.

Paine spoke first. "I may not understand everything you tell me, Betsy, but I do appreciate your responsiveness. If I had assigned this project to the Investment Committee, it would be weeks before I would see anything, and they would probably spend $75,000 in consulting fees. Let's see what you've come up with."

Betsy began by briefly reviewing the efficient asset mixes and the concepts upon which they were based, choosing her words very carefully so as to appeal to Paine's intuition. Then she reviewed yesterday's assignment as she understood it. Paine nodded in agreement with her understanding of the assignment. Finally, she showed him the results of her probability analysis.

Efficient Asset Mixes

	1	2	3	4	5	6	7
Stock (percent)	2.4	10.3	20.2	30.1	42.9	71.4	100.0
Bond (percent)	2.2	15.2	31.5	47.8	57.1	28.6	0.0
Short term (percent)	95.4	74.5	48.3	22.1	0.0	0.0	0.0
Expected return (percent)	7.2	8.0	9.0	10.0	11.0	12.0	13.0
Standard deviation (percent)	1.9	3.2	6.0	9.0	12.0	16.1	21.0

Probability of Exceeding −5 Percent

In any one year (percent)	99	99	99	95	91	85	80
On average over investment horizon (percent)	99	99	99	99	99	99	97
Each and every year (percent)	99	99	95	79	62	46	34

"Fascinating," said Paine. "It doesn't seem to matter what we do if we take a long-term view as long as our only concern is not losing more than 5 percent. Do I understand this table correctly, Betsy?"

"That's right. If your horizon is sufficiently long and you are not concerned with interim results, even a risky strategy, such as all stocks, provides virtual certainty of achieving a −5 percent return. In fact, if your horizon is long enough, a very risky strategy for the short term will have a higher downside return than a low-risk strategy over the long term, because return increases roughly with time while risk increases with the square root of time."

"You're starting to lose me, Betsy," said Paine. "Let's focus on the issue at hand and we'll talk about the square root of time some other day."

Betsy was annoyed at herself for her momentary lapse. She recovered quickly, though, and asked Paine if any of the asset mixes seemed to satisfy his requirement for exceeding −5 percent and his desire to maximize the fund's expected return.

"I think we should focus on the single year results," Paine said. "It won't do us any good to lose 5 percent in the first year and make 20 percent the second year, since the accountants keep score every year. Furthermore, I don't think we need to pay too much attention to satisfying the objective each and every year for the next five years. We can always revisit the analysis next year and so on. Our required return in future years will probably change anyway. The annual results suggest to me that we ought to adopt asset mix 4. If I understand your analysis, this mix has only a 1 in 20 chance of returning less than −5 percent and it is expected to return 10 percent per year."

"That's right," Betsy responded. "If you allocate 30 percent of the fund to stocks, 48 percent to bonds, and 22 percent to short-term securities, you can be very confident of achieving at least −5 percent and you can expect to achieve 10 percent."

"Well, personally, I would prefer a larger commitment to stocks, but

I can't ignore the consequences that such a strategy might have for our financial statements." Paine continued. "It seems as though we are forever compromising our long-term goals to satisfy our shareholders' demand for short-term profits." Then Paine turned to Betsy. "You've done a great job! I want you to prepare a report for the Investment Committee and present it at the next meeting. Be sure to emphasize our concern about the balance sheet. I'll be there to lend my support, but I want you to cover the details. I'm sure Patrick won't mind. And by the way, Betsy, Patrick was right when he suggested that you needed to be challenged more."

As Betsy left Paine's office she was delighted with the outcome and enthusiastic about next month's meeting. Soon her enthusiasm waned, however. "What will happen to the pension fund surplus if interest rates fall?" she wondered. "Won't the value of the pension liabilities increase if the benefit obligations are discounted by a lower rate?" She vaguely remembered that the new pension accounting rules dealt with valuation as well as disclosure. She made a mental note to discuss this concern with Patrick.

To be continued . . .

NOTE

1. This approach should not be used in situations in which there are more than three asset classes, since it is possible that the efficient portfolio includes a positive weight in the asset class that would have been sold short when the other asset classes are weighted differently.

PART 2

INNOVATIONS

In Part 2 we describe two important innovations to asset allocation: the introduction of liabilities to the asset allocation problem and hedging currency exposure from foreign investments.

Chapter 5 describes how to adapt strategic asset allocation to incorporate liabilities. The important insight is that the present value of liabilities, just as the present value of assets, changes stochastically with the passage of time rather than predictably. Therefore, liabilities can be treated as an asset with a fixed negative weight. Moreover, since some liabilities such as pension benefit obligations tend to have long durations, long-term bonds and even stocks in some circumstances tend to be less risky than Treasury bills in this augmented context of assets and liabilities.

In Chapter 6 we show how to adapt dynamic hedging strategies to incorporate liabilities. Again, within this broader context of the asset allocation issue, Treasury bills are not a riskless asset, since they do not track changes in the value of the liabilities as well as other assets. In fact, we show that a conventional portfolio insurance strategy that shifts a portfolio between stocks and Treasury bills, for example, increases rather than reduces the volatility of a pension fund's surplus value.

Chapter 7 deals with currency risk that emanates from foreign investments. Although global diversification typically improves a portfolio's efficiency in terms of expected return and risk, it does not necessarily follow that the part of a foreign asset's return due to conversion to the domestic currency benefits a portfolio. Unless we expect a currency to appreciate in value beyond the cost of hedging it, the volatility from exchange rate uncertainty will usually increase a portfolio's risk without a compensatory increase in expected return. Nonetheless, it is not usually optimal to hedge currency exposure fully. To the extent that currency returns are not perfectly correlated with each other, the foreign asset's local return, and the return of the domestic asset, we can lower portfolio risk beyond the level achieved by full hedging by tempering the percent of the currency exposure we hedge. The precise solution to this problem is described in Chapter 7.

CHAPTER 5

STRATEGIC ASSET ALLOCATION WITH LIABILITIES

INTRODUCTION

In our presentation of strategic asset allocation in Chapter 1, we showed how to apply portfolio theory to identify efficient asset mixes and how to evaluate these asset mixes according to their likelihood of achieving various return objectives. In the pension fund story, we introduced the notion that an important return objective is the level of return required to meet future benefit obligations. This example, however, oversimplified the problem by ignoring the uncertainty that surrounds the future valuation of pension liabilities and the intertemporal tradeoff between hedging near-term liabilities versus more distant liabilities. In this chapter we relax the assumption that pension liabilities are fixed or that their value changes predictably. Furthermore, we address the long-term cost of hedging near-term liabilities.

THE VALUATION OF PENSION LIABILITIES

In 1986, the Financial Accounting Standards Board promulgated Financial Accounting Standard No. 87 (FAS No. 87), establishing new pension accounting rules for corporate pension funds. Under FAS No. 87, if pension liabilities exceed pension assets, the shortfall must be reflected on the balance sheet as a liability. Moreover, companies are required to value liabilities at market, reflecting prevailing levels of interest rates.[1] These reporting and valuation changes help focus attention on the underlying economics of pension fund finance and reveal some seemingly strange notions. In the context of FAS No. 87, for example, Treasury bills are riskier than bonds and sometimes are as risky as stocks. In order to understand this counterintuitive notion, let us review a simple model for asset valuation and show its correspondence to the valuation of pension liabilities.

We can express the present value of a stream of cash flows as shown in Formula 5–1.

Formula 5–1   Present Value of Cash Flow Stream

$$P = \frac{C_1}{(1 + k)} + \frac{C_2}{(1 + k)^2} + \frac{C_3}{(1 + k)^3} + \ldots + \frac{C_n}{(1 + k)^n}$$

where

P = Present value of cash flows
C_1 = Cash flow in period 1
C_2 = Cash flow in period 2
C_3 = Cash flow in period 3
C_n = Cash flow in final period
k = Discount rate

If the asset is a stock, the cash flows are dividends and the stock's sale price. If the asset is a bond, the cash flows are coupons and sale price, or principal if the bond is prepaid or held to maturity. In the context of pension liabilities, the cash flows are benefit payments. This simple model captures the essence of valuation, for we can readily see that present value varies as the cash flows or the discount rate varies.

Inflation affects both the cash flows and the discount rate. The net effect depends on the differential effect of inflation on the discount rate and the growth rate of cash flows. If the inflation-induced change in the growth rate of the cash flows is sufficient to offset the change in the discount rate, present value will not be affected. If the inflation that is passed through to the cash flows is less than the increase in the discount rate, present value will decrease and vice versa. Present value is also affected by productivity gains, which increase present value by increasing cash flows, while it is affected inversely by fluctuations in the interest rate used to discount the cash flows.

WHY TREASURY BILLS ARE RISKY

Why are Treasury bills riskier than bonds and almost as risky as stocks? To the extent that the cash flows occur far into the future, the present value of these cash flows is more sensitive to changes in discount rates because the impact of the discount rate is felt for a longer period of time. Duration measures the average time to receipt of an asset's cash flows weighted by present value. Long-term assets such as stocks and bonds have relatively long durations. Short-term assets such as Treasury bills have a very short duration and are therefore relatively insensitive to changes in the discount rate. The present value of pension liabilities, for the most part, reflects the discounted value of benefit obligations that are due many years into the future. Hence, pension liabilities have a relatively long duration. Therefore, when interest rates rise, the present values of both long-term assets and liabilities fall. Similarly, when interest rates fall, their values rise. The response of asset values to changes in interest rates is apparent because these assets are traded daily. Pension liabilities, however, are not traded except occasionally in corporate restructurings or plan terminations. Nonetheless, their true economic value changes inversely with interest rates every day. From this perspective, long-term assets, to some extent, naturally hedge pension liabilities. Short-term assets, on the other hand, are relatively invariant to changes in interest rates so that they do not offset changes in the present value of liabilities.

In the context of assets and liabilities as formalized by FAS No. 87, risk is defined as the net volatility of pension assets and liabilities; that is, the volatility of the pension fund surplus.

Specifically, the net risk of pension assets and liabilities is computed as shown by Formula 5–2.[2]

Formula 5–2   Net Risk of Assets and Liabilities

$$S_N = \sqrt{S_A{}^2 + S_L{}^2 - 2 \cdot r \cdot S_A \cdot S_L}$$

where

S_N = Net standard deviation of assets and liabilities

S_A = Standard deviation of assets

S_L = Standard deviation of liabilities

r = Correlation coefficient of assets and liabilities

From this expression we can easily see that net risk decreases as the correlation between assets and liabilities increases, controlling for the standard deviations of assets and liabilities. To demonstrate that Treasury bills and other short-term securities may be riskier than stocks or bonds, suppose that the following relationships characterize the riskiness of assets and liabilities.

	Standard Deviation	Correlation with Liabilities
Stocks	15%	50%
Bonds	9%	90%
Short-term securities	1%	−15%
Liabilities	10%	100%

By substituting these values into Formula 5–2 we can estimate the net standard deviation for a portfolio of assets and liabilities depending on whether the assets are invested in stocks, bonds, or short-term securities. The values shown in Table 5–1 assume that the values of the assets and liabilities are equal.

Based on our assumptions, Table 5–1 shows that net risk is lowest if the assets are invested in bonds, while it is highest if the assets are invested in stocks. However, the net risk of a portfolio whose assets are invested in short-term securities is almost as risky as an all-stock portfolio, even though, in an absolute sense, short-term securities have a substantially lower standard deviation than stocks (1 percent versus 15 percent).

TABLE 5–1
Net Risk of Assets and Liabilities

Allocation of Assets	Net Standard Deviation of Assets and Liabilities
Stocks	13.23%
Bonds	4.36%
Short-term securities	10.20%

THE EFFICIENT FRONTIER WITH LIABILITIES

In Chapter 1, we showed how to identify efficient asset mixes assuming investment in stocks, bonds, and short-term securities. But if we view this problem in the context of both assets and liabilities, we discover that an asset mix that is efficient in the context of assets only is not necessarily efficient when we include liabilities. In order to estimate a portfolio's net expected return and net standard deviation, we simply include the liabilities as a negative asset in our calculations. Within this framework, a portfolio's expected return net of liabilities is computed as shown in Formula 5–3.

Formula 5–3   Expected Return of Portfolio of Assets and Liabilities (Two Assets)

$$R_N = R_1 \cdot W_1 + R_2 \cdot W_2 + R_L \cdot W_L$$

where

R_N = Net expected return of portfolio of assets and liabilities

R_1 = Expected return of asset 1

R_2 = Expected return of asset 2

R_L = Expected return of liabilities

W_1 = Percentage invested in asset 1

W_2 = Percentage invested in asset 2

W_L = Liabilities as a percent of total portfolio value (enter as a negative value)

We can use the same procedure to calculate the net standard deviation of a portfolio of assets and liabilities. Again, we simply include the liabilities as a negative asset. For example, the standard deviation of a portfolio consisting of two assets and a pool of liabilities is computed as shown in Formula 5–4.

Formula 5–4 Standard Deviation of Portfolio of Assets and Liabilities (Two Assets)

$$S_N = \sqrt{ \begin{array}{l} S_1^2 \cdot W_1^2 + S_2^2 \cdot W_2^2 + S_L^2 \cdot W_L^2 + \\ 2 \cdot r_{1,2} \cdot S_1 \cdot W_1 \cdot S_2 \cdot W_2 + \\ 2 \cdot r_{1,L} \cdot S_1 \cdot W_1 \cdot S_L \cdot W_L + \\ 2 \cdot r_{2,L} \cdot S_2 \cdot W_2 \cdot S_L \cdot W_L \end{array} }$$

where

S_N = Net standard deviation of portfolio of assets and liabilities

S_1 = Standard deviation of asset 1

S_2 = Standard deviation of asset 2

S_L = Standard deviation of liabilities

W_1 = Percentage invested in asset 1

W_2 = Percentage invested in asset 2

W_L = Liabilities as a percentage of total portfolio value (enter as a negative value)

$r_{1,2}$ = Correlation coefficient between asset 1 and asset 2

$r_{1,L}$ = Correlation coefficient between asset 1 and liabilities

$r_{2,L}$ = Correlation coefficient between asset 2 and liabilities

Unless the liabilities are independent of each of the assets, the asset weights that form the portfolios along the efficient frontier net of liabilities will differ from those that we obtain when we ignore liabilities. This fact precludes us from approaching portfolio optimization sequentially. For example, it is not correct to identify efficient asset mixes without consideration of liabilities as a preliminary step and subsequently introduce liabilities in order to estimate a portfolio's net expected return and net standard deviation. Although this approach yields correct estimates of net expected return and net standard deviation for each portfolio, it does so for the wrong portfolios.

For example, suppose we wish to construct a portfolio of stocks, bonds, and short-term securities with the following expected returns, standard deviations, and correlations:

	Expected Return	Standard Deviation	Correlation	
			Stocks	Bonds
Stocks	12.0%	15.0%		
Bonds	9.5%	9.0%	30.0%	
Short-term securities	7.0%	1.0%	−10.0%	10.0%

The minimum-risk portfolio with an expected return of 10 percent has a standard deviation of 7.85 percent and consists of 37.82 percent stocks, 44.35 percent bonds, and 17.83 percent short-term securities. This portfolio is efficient in the context of stocks, bonds, and short-term securities, since there is no other portfolio that has an expected return equal to or greater than 10 percent that is less risky (if we disallow short sales). What happens if we introduce liabilities? Suppose that liabilities have an expected return of 8 percent and a standard deviation of 10 percent. Further, suppose that liabilities are 50 percent correlated with stocks, 90 percent correlated with bonds, and −15 percent correlated with short-term securities. Finally, suppose that the present value of the liabilities equals 100 percent of the current asset value. The efficient asset mix of 37.82 percent stocks, 44.35 percent bonds, and 17.83 percent short-term securities has a net expected return of 2.0 percent and a net standard deviation of 5.80 percent. Is this portfolio efficient in terms of net return and net risk? Obviously, the answer is no or we would not have posed the question. A portfolio that is invested 20 percent in stocks and 80 percent in bonds has the same net expected return of 2.0 percent, yet it has a lower net standard deviation of 3.77 percent.

The message we wish to convey with this example is that liabilities should not be included as an afterthought when identifying efficient asset mixes. They should be included in the analysis right from the start and treated as a negative asset.

THE INTERTEMPORAL TRADEOFF

One of the most important notions in mean-variance analysis is that return increases approximately with time while risk increases approximately with the square root of time. It is this notion that explains why bonds, in the context of assets and liabilities, are less risky than stocks if our horizon is short, but as risky as or riskier than stocks if our horizon is long.

Behind this notion is the fact that as we extend our investment horizon, the dominant source of risk shifts from interest rate fluctuations to growth in cash flows. Over the short run, cash flows grow very little, while interest rates can fluctuate substantially. As we extend our horizon, though, interest rate fluctuations tend to cancel each other out while the growth in cash flows compounds. Since the cash flows of both stocks and liabilities grow with inflation and productivity gains, while the cash flows of bonds are fixed, stocks are usually a better long-term hedge for liabilities than are bonds.

SUMMARY

- The present value of liabilities is not constant. It changes as cash flow obligations change and as the rate used to discount these obligations changes.
- Since pension liabilities typically have long durations, long-term assets such as stocks and bonds are a better hedge for liabilities than are short-term securities; hence, in the context of net expected return and net risk, Treasury bills are riskier than bonds and almost as risky as stocks.
- We can identify efficient portfolios in the context of net expected return and net risk by treating liabilities as a "negative asset" in our portfolio optimization process. If we first identify the efficient portfolios without considering liabilities and subsequently introduce liabilities into our analysis, we will most likely select an inefficient portfolio in terms of net expected return and net risk.
- Over the short term, bonds are a better hedge for liabilities than are stocks, because interest rate fluctuations are the predominant source of risk. Over the long term, however, stocks are a better liability hedge than bonds, because the predominant risk is inadequate growth in cash flows.

NOTES

1. The provisions of Financial Accounting Standard No. 87 are described in, *Statement of Financial Accounting Standards No. 87—Employers' Accounting*

for Pensions (Stamford, Conn.: Financial Accounting Standards Board of the Financial Accounting Foundation, December 1985).
2. This formula assumes that the value of the liabilities equals the value of the assets.

CHAPTER 6

DYNAMIC HEDGING STRATEGIES
WITH LIABILITIES

INTRODUCTION

In Chapter 5, we proposed the notion that asset allocation decisions should reflect, at least to some extent, the interrelationship between the assets and the liabilities which the assets are intended to fund. In the case of a pension fund, for example, the pension liabilities should be regarded as a negative asset. The consequent investment results of viewing the assets in isolation are suboptimal when viewed from the broader perspective of both assets and liabilities. In fact, the Financial Accounting Standards Board (FASB) has lent credence to the notion that pension investment decisions should be based on consideration of both assets and liabilities. Corporate pension plan sponsors are now required to reflect underfunding of pension liabilities on the balance sheet as well as the income statement. Moreover, the valuation of pension liabilities must be in accordance with the prevailing market level of interest rates.[1] Although these specific disclosure and valuation requirements pertain only to corporate pension funds, the underlying economic concept applies to any investment situation where funds are set aside to fund either explicit or implicit liabilities. Hence, this notion applies to public pension funds, endowment funds, foundations, and even personal savings.

In Chapter 3, we introduced a dynamic hedging strategy called portfolio insurance. We showed that by shifting our fund between a risky asset and a riskless asset, we could ensure that our fund would not fall below some prespecified value and, in the event the risky asset appreciated, we could capture a preponderance of the risky asset's gain. Portfolio insurance, when viewed in the context of both assets and liabilities, however, has a perverse consequence when it is applied only to the assets. Instead of reducing the uncertainty of the pension fund's net worth,[2] it increases its uncertainty. Ironically, a strategy that was designed to control pension investment risk, in many applications, actually exacerbates risk. Let us demonstrate this strange notion with an example. Suppose that we implement a portfolio insurance strategy to ensure that a $100 fund will not fall below $95 one year from now regardless of the performance of the risky asset. We choose this floor value because our liabilities are currently valued at $95. Let us also assume that the approximate cost of this protection is 3 percent. In other words, if the risky asset should increase in value we will capture only 97 percent of its terminal value. Recall from Chapter 5 that over short investment horizons the predominant source of risk is uncertainty in discount rates and that this risk is common to both assets and liabilities. Now suppose that the duration of our liabilities is longer than the duration of our assets, so that the liabilities are more sensitive to changes in interest rates. Specifically, let us assume that the value of the liabilities changes 7 percent for a 100-basis point move in interest rates while the asset value changes only 5 percent for a 100-basis point move in interest rates.

What happens if interest rates rise by 150 basis points? Had we not insured our risky portfolio, it would have decreased in value to $92.50 [$100 − 5 · 1.5]. Since we insured it, though, we end up with $95, our insured value. At the same time, the liabilities would have fallen to $84.50 [$95 − 7 · 1.5]. In this situation, the insurance helped because the ratio of our assets to liabilities increased from 1.05 ($100/$95) to 1.12 ($95/$84.50). Had we not insured our assets, our asset/liability ratio at the end of the year would have been only 1.09 ($92.50/$84.50).

Now consider what happens if interest rates decline by 150 basis points. In this scenario, had we not implemented the portfolio insurance strategy, our risky portfolio would have increased in value to $107.50 ($100 + $5 · 1.5). Since we insured it, though, it grew to only 97 percent of $107.50, or $104.28. Meanwhile, the liabilities rose from $95 to $105.50 ($95 + $7 · 1.5). Thus, our asset/liability ratio, instead of equaling 1.02 ($107.50/$105.50) at the end of our horizon, equals only .99 ($104.28/$105.50) as a result of our decision to insure the assets. Strangely, in a situation where the assets are insured, the ending asset/liability ratio is more uncertain given unpredictable interest rates than it is if we choose not to insure the assets. If the assets are insured, the asset/liability ratio ranges from .98 to 1.12. If, on the other hand, we choose not to insure the assets, the asset/liability ratio ranges from 1.01 to 1.09. These results are summarized in Table 6–1.

Of course, we are not restricted to a choice of insuring the assets or not insuring the assets. We may instead choose to insure a portfolio's net worth. We describe this strategy in the next section.

INSURING A PORTFOLIO'S NET WORTH

Just as we implement traditional portfolio insurance by shifting a fund between a risky asset and a riskless asset, we can protect the net worth of a fund by shifting between a risky asset and a riskless asset. And as with traditional portfolio insurance, we can invoke the theory of option valuation to determine the expected cost of the strategy and the amounts to shift as the fund value and the liability value change through time. However, in order to insure net worth, we must make two simple modifications to the Black-Scholes model.

Suppose we wish to ensure that the future value of a pension fund will equal or exceed some prespecified percentage of the uncertain future value

TABLE 6–1
The Effect of Portfolio Insurance on the Asset/Liability Ratio

	Starting Values	
Insured portfolio	$100.00	$100.00
Uninsured portfolio	$100.00	$100.00
Liabilities	$ 95.00	$ 95.00
Asset/liability ratio	1.05	1.05
	Ending Values	
	Interest Rates Increase 1.5%	Interest Rates Decrease 1.5%
Insured portfolio	$ 95.00	$104.28
Uninsured portfolio	$ 92.50	$107.50
Liabilities	$ 85.03	$106.25
Insured asset/liability ratio	1.12	.99
Uninsured asset/liability ratio	1.09	1.02

of the pension liabilities, regardless of how their values change in relation to each other. Moreover, should the value of the risky asset increase relative to the value of the pension liabilities, we will wish to capture as much of this relative increase as possible. Given how we framed this problem, the riskless asset is an asset or portfolio that moves exactly in concert with changes in the value of the liabilities. And, of course, a risky asset is any asset or portfolio that does not move perfectly with our liabilities. Therefore, as unlikely as it may seem, Treasury bills are a risky asset in this context.

Within this context, a perfectly riskless strategy is to invest our entire fund in an asset that mimics our liabilities. Such a strategy would ensure that our asset/liability ratio never changes. However, such a strategy would also ensure that we would not benefit from any favorable performance of the risky asset should it perform better than the liabilities. On the other hand, if we invested all of our assets in a risky asset, be it Treasury bills or some other asset that is at least partly uncorrelated with our liabilities, we risk the chance that our liabilities will increase more or decrease less than our assets. If we are starting from a position where our asset value exceeds the value of our liabilities, we may prefer a strategy that ensures that we achieve a minimum asset/liability ratio while allowing us to participate in the risky asset's potentially favorable relative performance.

As you might suspect by now, the modifications necessary for us to adapt the Black-Scholes model to our particular problem have to do with our definition of risk and the riskless return. The riskless return equals the return of the liability-mimicking asset net of the return of the liabilities. To the extent that this asset exactly matches the changes in the value of the liabilities, the riskless return equals 0 percent. And risk, in this context, equals the volatility of the differences in return between the risky asset and the liabilities. As we demonstrated in Chapter 5, we can compute this value, which we call net risk, as a function of the standard deviations of the risky asset and the liabilities and the correlation between the two. Specifically, we can express net risk as shown in Formula 6–1.

Formula 6–1   Net Risk

$$S_N = \sqrt{S_A^2 + S_L^2 - 2 \cdot r \cdot S_A \cdot S_L}$$

where

S_N = Net risk of assets and liabilities
S_A = Standard deviation of assets
S_L = Standard deviation of liabilities
r = Correlation coefficient between assets and liabilities

This formulation of net risk is equivalent to the standard deviation of a strategy whereby we invest a long position in the assets and sell short an equal position in the liabilities. We would also arrive at the same value if we first computed the differences in return between the assets and the liabilities and then computed the standard deviation of those values.

With these two changes, we can rewrite the Black-Scholes model as shown in Formula 6–2. This formula allows us to compute the value of an option to exchange one risky asset for another,[3] which is, in effect, what we wish to replicate—an option to exchange a risky asset for a liability-mimicking asset.

Formula 6–2   An Option to Exchange a Risky Asset for a Liability-Mimicking Asset

(1) $C = N(D1) \cdot R - N(D2) \cdot L$

(2) $D1 = \dfrac{ln(R/L) + 1/2 \cdot (S^2_R + S^2_L - 2 \cdot r \cdot S_R \cdot S_L) \cdot T}{(S^2_R + S^2_L - 2 \cdot r \cdot S_R + S_L)^{\frac{1}{2}} \cdot T^{\frac{1}{2}}}$

(3) $D2 = D1 - (S^2_R + S^2_L - 2 \cdot r \cdot S_R + S_L)^{\frac{1}{2}} \cdot T^{\frac{1}{2}}$

where

C = Option to exchange risky asset for liability-mimicking asset
R = Price of risky asset
L = Price of liability-mimicking asset
S_R = Standard deviation of risky asset
S_L = Standard deviation of liability-mimicking asset

r = Correlation between risky asset and liability-mimicking asset

T = Investment horizon

$N()$ = Cumulative normal density function

ln = Natural log

It should be obvious, when we compare Formula 6–2 to Formula 2–1 in Chapter 2, that we have simply substituted into the Black-Scholes equation the ratio of the risky asset and the liability-mimicking asset for the price of the risky asset, zero for the riskless rate of interest, and net risk for the standard deviation of the risky asset.

Now we can proceed (as described in Chapter 2) to determine the cost of insuring our fund's net worth and the appropriate amounts to allocate to the risky asset and the liability-mimicking asset. Suppose that our fund is currently invested in an equity index fund and that its value is $100 million, while the value of our liabilities equals $92 million. Thus, our asset/liability ratio equals 1.087. We wish to ensure that the value of our fund will not fall below 100 percent of our liabilities one year from now. And, of course, should equities increase in value relative to liabilities, we would like to capture as much of this favorable relative performance as possible. Suppose that the equity fund has a standard deviation of 20 percent, while the liabilities have a standard deviation of 15 percent, and that they are 50 percent correlated with each other. Finally, suppose we can invest in an asset that hedges our liabilities perfectly (liability-mimicking asset).

If we substitute these values in Formula 6–2, we find that a hypothetical (shadow) option to exchange our equity fund for a liability-mimicking asset would cost $11.62 million. And from put-call parity, we know that a hypothetical put option indexed to the value of our liabilities would cost $3.62 million (see Formula 2–2 in Chapter 2).

However, the same problem that we encountered with traditional portfolio insurance appears again. We cannot afford to invest $100 million dollars in a risky asset and another $3.62 million in a protective put option. Therefore, we must iteratively solve for the value of a risky asset and a put option so that in total they equal our $100 million of available funds. If we proceed in this fashion, we find that we can purchase $94.47 million of the risky asset, leaving $5.53 million to apply toward the purchase of a put option. But, of course, such an option does not exist. Therefore, we replicate this option by investing \$56.08 million ($N(D1) \cdot 94.47$) in our equity portfolio and \$43.92 million in the liability-mimicking portfolio. These calculations are shown below.

$$D1 = \frac{ln(94.47/92) + 1/2 \cdot (.2^2 + .15^2 - 2 \cdot .5 \cdot .2 \cdot .15)}{(.2^2 + .15^2 - 2 \cdot .5 \cdot .2 \cdot .15)^{\frac{1}{2}}} = .5527$$

$$D2 = .5527 - (.2^2 + .15^2 - 2 \cdot .5 \cdot .2 \cdot .15)^{\frac{1}{2}} = .3724$$

$$C = N(.5527) \cdot 94.47 - N(.3724) \cdot 92$$

$$C = .5936 \cdot 94.47 - .5226 \cdot 92 = 8.00$$

$$P = 8.00 - 94.47 + 92 = 5.53$$

As the values of our fund and our liabilities change and as we approach the end of our investment horizon, we must adjust the allocation to the risky asset and the liability-mimicking asset by repeating the valuation process we have just described (without iterating, though, since we know the value of the risky asset). If we follow this strategy precisely, trading as required by the changing hedge ratio, and if our estimates of risk and correlation are accurate, we will end up with a fund value equal to at least 100 percent of the liabilities at the end of our horizon, regardless of the relative performance of our assets and liabilities. Moreover, if the risky asset outperforms the liabilities, we should capture about 94.5 percent of the ending asset/liability ratio.

THE COMPARATIVE COST OF INSURING PORTFOLIO ASSETS VERSUS PORTFOLIO NET WORTH

By examining Formula 6–2, we see that the net risk of the risky asset and the liabilities depends on the standard deviation of the risky asset, the standard deviation of the liabilities, and their correlation with each other. Net risk unambiguously decreases as the correlation increases since the correlation is preceded by a negative sign. It may not be readily obvious, however, whether net risk increases or decreases as a function of the risky asset's standard deviation or the liabilities' standard deviation since these values appear twice in the formula, once as a positive value and once as a negative. If we were to take the partial derivative of net risk with respect to the risky asset's standard deviation and the liability's standard deviation, we would find that net risk increases as the difference in their standard deviations increases.[4] The intuition behind these mathematical relationships is really quite simple. To the extent the risky asset and the liabilities move together (high correlation, similar standard deviations), they hedge each other. Since a common source of risk for both liabilities and long-term assets, such as stocks and long-term bonds, is uncertainty in discount rates, they tend to move together, at least partially. Therefore, long-term assets and long-term liabilities naturally hedge each other.

The importance of this phenomenon is that options, and therefore strategies to replicate options, are more expensive the riskier is the underlying asset. The intuition here is obvious. The chance that an option will expire "in the money" increases as the range of potential values for the underlying asset increases. Therefore, if assets and liabilities are of similar risk and are positively correlated with each other, it may be less expensive to insure a fund's net worth than it is to insure the fund's asset value.

Table 6–2 compares the cost of traditional portfolio insurance with the cost of insuring a fund's net worth. In the case of traditional portfolio insurance, we assumed that the riskless rate of interest was 8 percent and that the standard deviation of the risky asset was 15 percent. In the case of insuring the net worth, we assumed that the standard deviation of the risky asset was 15 percent, the standard deviation of the liability-mimicking asset was 10 percent, and that the risky asset and the liabilities were 75 percent correlated with each other. The costs represent the shadow price of a protective put option as a percentage of portfolio value. The minimum required returns are expressed relative to the riskless return in the case of traditional portfolio insurance and the liability return (which is also the riskless return when viewed from the perspective of net worth) in the case of insuring the fund's net worth.

According to Table 6–2, it is less expensive to protect a fund's value as a percentage of the value of liabilities (funded ratio) than it is to protect a fund's absolute value. For example, if we have a one-year investment horizon and we wish to protect a fund from returning less than the riskless

TABLE 6–2
Traditional Portfolio Insurance versus Net Worth Insurance

Minimum Required Return (percent)	One Year		Two Years		Three Years	
	PI	NWI	PI	NWI	PI	NWI
−1	14.2	9.2	7.9	5.6	5.0	4.0
−2	10.9	6.5	5.6	3.6	3.2	2.4
−3	8.8	4.8	4.2	2.4	2.1	1.6
−4	7.2	3.7	3.2	1.7	1.4	1.0
−5	6.0	2.9	2.5	1.2	0.9	0.7

return minus 5 percent, the expected cost of this protection is 6 percent of terminal wealth. That is, if the risky asset increases 20 percent, from $100.00 to $120.00, we would expect our fund to increase to $112.80 ($120.00 · 94%). If, instead, we choose a strategy whereby we seek to protect our funded ratio from declining by more than 5 percent, we would expect this protection to cost only 2.9 percent. Thus, if we started out fully funded and the risky asset increased to 120 percent of the value of the liabilities, we would expect our funded ratio to increase to 116.52 percent (120.00% · 97.1%).

Of course, it may not always be the case that it is less expensive to insure a fund's net worth than its absolute value. The relative cost of these two strategies depends on the extent of the natural hedge between the risky asset and the liabilities, the riskiness of the risky asset, and the riskless return. In many if not most situations, it will be cheaper to insure the net worth than the asset value.

CONSTANT PROPORTION PORTFOLIO INSURANCE WITH LIABILITIES

In Chapter 2 we showed how we could capture the essence of portfolio insurance with a simple linear investment rule known as constant proportion portfolio insurance (CPPI). We can easily adapt this simple investment rule to protect the net worth of a fund.

The mechanics of CPPI are quite simple. All we need to do is specify a floor value and a multiple. The multiple must be greater than one, and the higher it is the more aggressive we are in pursuing the strategy. For example, suppose our fund is currently valued at $100 million and we choose a floor value of $85 million and a multiple of 5. In order to implement CPPI, we simply invest an amount equal to the fund value less the floor value (which is called the cushion) times the multiple in a risky asset and the balance in a riskless asset. Thus, in our example, we start out by investing $75 million [5 · ($100 – $85)] in a risky asset and $25 million in a riskless asset. If the fund value increases to $102 million, we raise our exposure to the risky asset to $85 million [5 · ($102 – $85)]. If, on the other hand, the fund value falls to $98 million, we reduce our risky exposure to $65 million [5 · ($98 – $85)]. This strategy will ensure that our fund value never falls below $85 million unless its value declines by a percentage greater than the reciprocal of the multiple between trades. For example, if the multiple is 5, then the fund would have to decline by more than 20 percent (1/5) in order to penetrate the floor.

With a very simple innovation, we can adapt CPPI to protect the net worth of a fund. We merely index the floor value to the net worth and shift the fund between a risky asset and a liability-mimicking asset. Suppose, for example, that the market value of our fund equals $115 million and the present value of our liabilities equals $100 million. If we wish to ensure that the fund's net worth will never be negative (net worth floor value equals 0), and we choose a multiple of 5, then we begin by allocating $75 million ($15 million · 5) to the risky asset and $40 million to the liability-mimicking asset. Now consider a situation in which the liabilities increase to $105 million while our fund value remains unchanged. Our net worth cushion changed from $15 million to $10 million. Thus we need to reduce our exposure to the risky asset from $75 million to $50 million ($10 million · 5). If, instead, the value of our fund increases to $120 million while our liabilities decrease to $98 million, our net worth cushion increases to $22 million, and we increase our risky asset exposure to $110 million ($22 million · 5). Now imagine that both our portfolio value and our liabilities change by the same amount. In this case, the cushion remains constant so that we need not change our allocation to the risky asset. In Table 6–3, we demonstrate how to implement CPPI to protect a fund's net worth. Note that in some instances, when the fund value increases, the allocation to the risky asset declines because the liability value increased by a greater amount.

TABLE 6–3
CPPI with Liabilities

Net Worth Floor = 0
Multiple = 5

Fund Value	Liability Value	Net Worth Cushion	R.A. Allocation	L.M.A. Allocation	R.A. Return	L.M.A. Return
115.00	100.00	15.00	75.00	40.00	0.00%	7.50%
118.00	107.50	10.50	52.50	65.50	2.00%	−6.00%
115.12	101.05	14.07	70.35	44.77	5.00%	10.00%
123.11	111.16	11.96	59.80	63.32	10.00%	15.00%
138.59	127.83	10.76	53.82	84.77	−12.00%	20.00%
115.18	102.26	12.92	64.58	50.60		

The advantages of CPPI over traditional portfolio insurance apply as well when we include liabilities. Clearly, the strategy is less complex and more intuitively pleasing than traditional portfolio insurance. In addition, it is invariant to time so that we do not need to decide whether or not to restart the strategy at the end of a prespecified investment horizon. Moreover, we are not required to trade merely in response to the passage of time.

SUMMARY

- Portfolio insurance that protects the absolute value of a fund's assets usually has the perverse consequence of increasing the riskiness of the fund's net worth.
- As an alternative to insuring a fund's assets, we can insure a fund's net worth by replicating an option to exchange a risky asset for a liability-mimicking asset.
- Within the context of insuring a fund's net worth, a riskless asset is one that mimics the changes in the value of the liabilities, while a risky asset is any asset that is not perfectly correlated with the liabilities. Therefore, Treasury bills are risky relative to long-term liabilities.
- It is usually less expensive to insure a fund's net worth than to insure a fund's asset value because assets and liabilities are partly

correlated with each other and, therefore, naturally hedge each other. In other words, the net risk of assets and liabilities is typically less than the total risk of the assets.
- As an alternative to using an option-based approach to insure a fund's net worth, we can protect net worth with a simple variation of constant proportion portfolio insurance. We simply index the floor value to the fund's net worth and allocate our fund between a risky asset and a liability-mimicking asset.

NOTES

1. The provisions of Financial Accounting Standards No. 87 are described in: *Statement of Financial Accounting Standards No. 87—Employers' Accounting for Pensions* (Stamford, Conn.: Financial Accounting Standards Board of the Financial Accounting Foundation, December 1985).
2. Net worth in this context is defined as the value of the pension assets less the value of the pension liabilities. It is sometimes referred to as the pension fund surplus. Further, liabilities can be defined as the accumulated benefit obligation, which includes the vested and nonvested benefit obligation as of the present, or they can be defined as the projected benefit obligation, which, in addition to the accumulated benefit obligation, includes a projected benefit obligation reflecting the effect of future salary increases on past service and future service. The Financial Accounting Standards Board uses the accumulated benefit obligation for disclosure rules.
3. For a derivation of this formula, see W. Margrabe, "The Value of an Option to Exchange One Asset for Another," *Journal of Finance* (March 1978), pp. 177–188.
4. The partial derivative of net variance with respect to correlation equals:

$$\delta S^2_N / \delta r = -2 \cdot S_A \cdot S_L$$

The partial derivative of net variance with respect to the asset's standard deviation equals:

$$\delta S^2_N / \delta S_A = 2 \cdot S_A - 2 \cdot r \cdot S_L$$

The partial derivative of net variance with respect to the liability's standard deviation equals:

$$\delta S^2_N / \delta S_L = 2 \cdot S_L - 2 \cdot r \cdot S_A$$

where

S^2_N = Net variance

S_A = Standard deviation of assets

S_L = Standard deviation of liabilities

r = Correlation coefficient between assets and liabilities

CHAPTER 7

FOREIGN EXCHANGE RISK IN ASSET ALLOCATION

INTRODUCTION

Foreign diversification by institutional investors has expanded rapidly in recent years. An important motivation to invest in foreign markets stems from the principles of portfolio theory. Since foreign assets typically have a low correlation with domestic assets, investors can improve the efficiency of their portfolios by diversifying into foreign assets. It is not necessarily the case, however, that the concomitant exposure to foreign currencies is always beneficial. Clearly, there are periods in which exposure to foreign currency improves performance, but there are also periods when it would have been better to hedge away currency exposure. Since the standard practice historically has been to accept the currency risk that goes along with foreign investment, and since foreign investment over the long run has typically improved performance, it may be tempting to assume that exposure to foreign currency is beneficial. There is an important distinction, however, between investment in a foreign asset and investment in a foreign currency. The foreign asset typically represents a productive resource that generates a growing stream of income. Since the present value of this income stream has a low correlation with the present value of income streams generated by domestic assets, it is usually beneficial to diversify into foreign assets. Currencies, however, reflect the relative productivity of countries. Sometimes a particular country is relatively productive and sometimes it is relatively unproductive. Thus, over the long run, whereas we should expect a foreign asset to generate a positive return, we should expect the return of its country's currency to equal 0 percent. The currency's actual return may turn out to be very high or very low, and we may even be justified in expecting a substantially non-zero return over some finite period. Nonetheless, the average currency over the long run should produce a return close to 0 percent, while the average asset over the long run should generate a return commensurate with its systematic risk.[1]

Suppose we are ambivalent about currency returns over our investment horizon and we accept the argument that 0 percent is a valid default assumption. Should we be indifferent between hedging or exposing our fund to currency risk? Although currencies have an expected return of 0 percent, their risk is non-zero. Thus, if we were to accept full currency exposure, we might accept risk without compensation. Unless we believe that a currency will generate a return sufficient to compensate for the risk it adds to our fund, we should hedge at least some of the currency exposure by selling futures or forward contracts. (Even if we expect a non-zero return for a currency, it is more efficient to separate the currency exposure decision from the country allocation decision.[2])

In order to focus on these issues, suppose that there are two assets available for investment, a domestic asset and a foreign asset. Suppose that both assets have an expected return of 12 percent and a standard deviation of 20 percent and that they are uncorrelated with each other (denominated in the domestic currency). Further, suppose that the foreign currency exposure that is embedded in our exposure to the foreign asset has an expected return of 0 percent with a standard deviation of 10 percent and that it is uncorrelated with the domestic asset and 50 percent correlated with the foreign asset. (We should expect the currency to be positively correlated with the foreign asset, since part of the foreign asset's return denominated in the domestic currency is the currency's return.) These assumptions are shown below:

	Expected Return (percent)	Standard Deviation (percent)	Correlation	
			Domestic Asset (percent)	Foreign Asset (percent)
Domestic asset	12	20		
Foreign asset	12	20	0	
Foreign currency	0	10	0	50

Suppose we allocate our fund equally between the domestic asset and the foreign asset and we do not hedge our embedded currency exposure. This allocation will result in an expected return of 12 percent with a standard deviation of 14.14 percent for the total portfolio. Thus the internationally diversified portfolio is superior to both the domestic asset and the foreign asset. The diversified portfolio has the same expected return as both assets but a lower standard deviation. Now consider what happens if we hedge the fund's exposure to the foreign currency. The fund's return remains unchanged at 12 percent, but its standard deviation falls to 13.23 percent. These results are summarized in Table 7–1.

Proponents of international diversification normally cite the reduction in risk associated with foreign investment to bolster their position, but very seldom do they pursue this argument to its logical conclusion with respect to currency exposure.

COMPLETE HEDGING VERSUS OPTIMAL HEDGING

Suppose we accept the view that we should hedge some of the currency exposure associated with our foreign investment. How should we proceed? As a first approximation, we might simply sell currency futures or forward contracts in an amount equal to the value of our foreign investment. As the value of our investment changes over time, we would adjust our currency position accordingly. Thus, we would always be fully hedged.

Although this approach eliminates currency risk, it does not necessarily yield the least risky portfolio. It may be the case that the currencies

TABLE 7–1
The Effect of Foreign Diversification and Currency Hedging on Portfolio Risk

	Expected Return (percent)	Standard Deviation (percent)
Domestic asset	12	20.00
Foreign asset	12	20.00
Unhedged portfolio	12	14.14
Hedged - portfolio	12	13.23

are correlated with each other and with the domestic and foreign assets in such a way that we could reduce the risk of our total portfolio even further by explicitly accounting for the specific correlation structure among the currencies and assets.

To focus on this issue, let us again assume that we invest our fund equally between a domestic asset and a foreign asset, each of which has an expected return of 12 percent and a standard deviation of 20 percent. Further, let us again assume that the foreign currency has a standard deviation of 10 percent, is uncorrelated with the domestic asset, and is 50 percent correlated with the foreign asset. In Figure 7–1, we show the total portfolio risk as a function of the percent of the currency exposure that is hedged. (In this example, percent hedged is relative to the exposure to the foreign asset, not the total portfolio.) In the case in which the currency

FIGURE 7–1
Minimum Risk Portfolio: 100% Hedged

	Expected Return	Standard Deviation	Correlation Domestic Asset	Correlation Foreign Asset
Domestic asset	12%	20%		
Foreign asset	12%	20%	0%	
Foreign currency	0%	10%	0%	50%

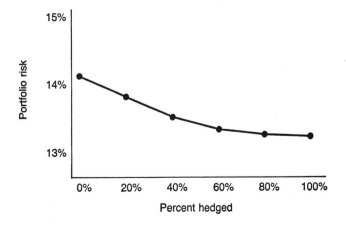

moves independently of the domestic asset but is 50 percent correlated with the foreign asset, it is optimal to hedge the embedded currency exposure fully.

Next we assume that the foreign currency is uncorrelated with both the domestic asset and the foreign asset and that the domestic and foreign assets are uncorrelated with each other. We retain our assumptions regarding expected return and standard deviation. With this correlation structure, the minimum risk portfolio is achieved at the point where the portfolio is fully exposed to the foreign currency, as shown in Figure 7–2.

Now let us assume that the foreign currency is uncorrelated with the domestic asset and 30 percent postively correlated with the foreign asset and that the domestic and foreign assets are uncorrelated with each other,

FIGURE 7–2
Minimum Risk Portfolio: 0% Hedged

	Expected Return	Standard Deviation	Correlation Domestic Asset	Correlation Foreign Asset
Domestic asset	12%	20%		
Foreign asset	12%	20%	0%	
Foreign currency	0%	10%	0%	50%

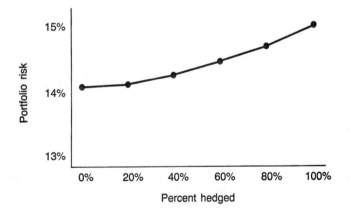

FIGURE 7–3
Minimum Risk Portfolio: 60% Hedged

	Expected Return	Standard Deviation	Correlation Domestic Asset	Correlation Foreign Asset
Domestic asset	12%	20%		
Foreign asset	12%	20%	0%	
Foreign exchange	0%	10%	0%	30%

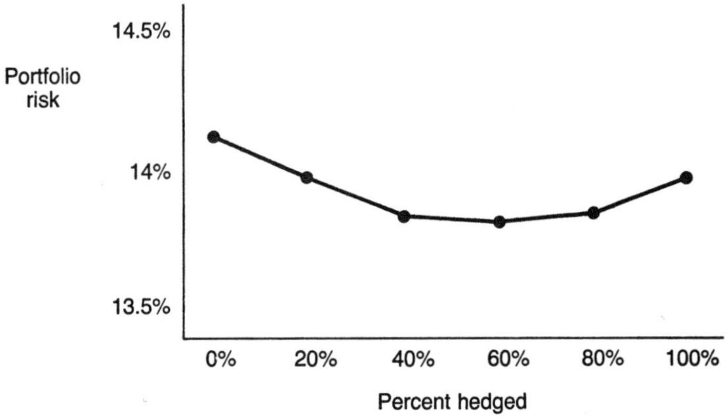

again retaining our other assumptions as to expected return and standard deviation. In this case, the portfolio risk is minimized if we hedge 60 percent of the embedded currency exposure, as shown in Figure 7–3.

These examples are grossly oversimplified. In a typical portfolio that is diversified internationally, there may be several asset classes in each foreign country and several foreign countries in which we invest our fund. Thus we would need to specify the correlation between every pair of assets, between every currency and every asset, and between every pair of currencies. Our oversimplified examples are intended to demonstrate the fact that, in the context of foreign diversification, complete hedging does not necessarily yield the least risky or optimal portfolio. Instead, it depends on the specific correlation structure among the currencies and assets.

A SIMPLE ALGORITHM FOR OPTIMAL CURRENCY HEDGING

In general, we can determine the optimal amount of our currency exposure to hedge by adapting an algorithm presented by William Sharpe in a 1978 working paper entitled, "An Algorithm for Portfolio Improvement."[3] Sharpe's algorithm was designed to determine the optimal weights for a portfolio of securities. He showed that in a mean-variance context, we can improve our utility by increasing our portfolio's exposure to a security if the derivative of our objective function with respect to this security is positive and by decreasing exposure to a security if the derivative is negative. When all of the derivatives are equal to each other, the portfolio is allocated optimally across the securities (see Appendix A).

In order to adapt Sharpe's algorithm to currency hedging, we need to make two modifications. First, we assume that the weights of the underlying assets are fixed and sum to 1. This assumption allows us to ignore the expected returns of the underlying assets as well as the covariances between each pair of assets. Second, we impose the constraint that each currency exposure independent of the embedded exposure from the foreign asset ranges from a minimum value equal to −1 times the exposure of the foreign asset (fully hedged) to a maximum value equal to 0 percent of the portfolio value (fully exposed). These exposures, unlike the asset weights need not sum to 1. This constraint simply implies that we cannot have a net long or a net short position in a currency, which is a typical constraint for most institutional investors.

We will demonstrate our algorithm with a simple case in which we have a portfolio that includes a single domestic asset and a single foreign asset. We assume that we wish to maximize our utility. Thus we can define our objective function in the usual form as shown in Formula 7–1.

Formula 7–1   Currency Hedging Objective Function

$$
\begin{aligned}
z = {} & R_D W_D + R_F W_F + R_C W_C - \lambda \, (S^2_D W^2_D + S^2_F W^2_F \\
& + S^2_C W^2_C + 2r_{D,F} \, S_D W_D S_F W_F + 2r_{D,C} S_D W_D S_C W_C \\
& + 2r_{F,C} S_F W_F S_C W_C)
\end{aligned}
$$

where

z = Objective function

R_D = Expected return of domestic asset

R_F = Expected return of foreign asset *denominated in domestic currency*

R_C = Expected return of foreign currency

W_D = Percent of portfolio allocated to domestic asset

W_F = Percent of portfolio allocated to foreign asset

W_C = Percent of portfolio allocated to foreign currency *independent of embedded exposure from foreign asset*

S_D = Standard deviation of domestic asset

S_F = Standard deviation of foreign asset

S_C = Standard deviation of foreign currency

$r_{D,F}$ = Correlation between domestic asset and foreign asset

$r_{D,C}$ = Correlation between domestic asset and foreign currency

$r_{F,C}$ = Correlation between foreign asset and foreign currency

λ = Risk aversion

and subject to

$\quad$ (1) $\quad W_D + W_F = 1$ and are fixed

$\quad$ (2) $\quad -W_F \leq W_C \leq 0$

Next, we simply take the derivative of our objective function with respect to W_C, the allocation to the foreign currency measured as a percent of the total portfolio, as shown in Formula 7–2.

Formula 7–2 Sensitivity of Utility to Currency Exposure

$$\delta z \delta \ W_C = R_C - \lambda \ (2S^2{}_C W_C + 2r_{D,C} S_D W_D S_C + 2r_{F,C} S_F W_F S_C)$$

This simple expression reflects the sensitivity of our utility to our portfolio's exposure to the foreign currency. If its value is negative, we can increase our utility by lowering the exposure to the foreign currency, while a positive value indicates that we can increase our utility by raising the exposure to the foreign currency. Remember that exposure in this context is independent of the embedded currency exposure associated with our foreign asset, and that it ranges from −1 times the foreign asset exposure (fully hedged) to 0 (fully exposed). When the derivative or sensitivity equals 0, we cannot increase our utility by changing the currency exposure. Thus we iteratively change the currency exposure until the sensitivity equals 0 or until we have reached the upper or lower constraint for the currency exposure. (Since the currency exposures need not sum to 1, we achieve optimality when the derivatives equal 0 rather than when they equal each other, subject to our constraints.)

The algorithm presented above is fairly general in that it allows for non-zero expected returns, multiple foreign assets, and a variety of constraints. In some special cases, however, the optimal hedging strategy can be derived in a more direct manner.

Suppose, for example, that our portfolio includes a single foreign asset and that we wish to minimize portfolio risk or, alternatively, that we believe the foreign currency's expected return equals 0 percent. In this case, the optimal weight for the foreign currency equals minus one times the currency's beta with respect to the underlying portfolio.

Now suppose our portfolio includes several foreign assets with varying correlations between each pair of currencies. In order to arrive at an exact solution, we must account for these varying correlations. If we wish merely to minimize risk, or if we assume that the currencies have expected returns equal to 0 percent, and if we *do not* constrain the exposures to the currencies, we can determine the optimal hedging strategy through multiple-regression analysis. We simply set the dependent variable equal to the return of the underlying portfolio and the independent variables equal to the returns of the relevant currencies. The resulting coefficient for each currency times minus one equals the optimal exposure for the currency.

NOMINAL HEDGING VERSUS REAL HEDGING

So far in our discussion of currency hedging, we have assumed implicitly that we wish to minimize portfolio risk in nominal terms. Some investors have argued against hedging currency risk because they believe that exposure to foreign exchange offers protection from inflation induced by consumption of foreign products. This line of reasoning proceeds as follows. Suppose we allocate our savings equally among U.S. assets, German assets, and Japanese assets and we intend to purchase a German-manufactured automobile and electronic equipment made in Japan. Now suppose we hedge the embedded currency exposure of our portfolio, and the dollar subsequently depreciates against the German mark and the Japanese yen. Our savings do not benefit from the dollar's decline since we hedged away our exposure to the foreign currencies that have risen relative to the dollar. Moreover, we now must spend more of our dollars to purchase our automobile and electronic equipment. If instead of hedging our currency exposure, we left our savings fully exposed to the embedded currency exposure of our foreign investment, our savings would have appreciated as the dollar declined, thereby partly offsetting the inflated prices which we now must pay for our new automobile and electronic equipment.

Although this line of reasoning has merit, it does not invalidate our hedging algorithm. Clearly, to the extent that consumption of foreign products affects our unique rate of inflation, the argument to hedge away currency risk diminishes. However, if our consumption of foreign products is only a small part of our total consumption, it is quite likely that the inflation-hedged properties of currencies are not sufficient to compensate for the incremental uncertainty associated with exposure to currencies. In any event, if we are concerned about the purchasing power of our portfolio, we should define our asset and currency returns after inflation and base our estimates of expected return, standard deviation, and correlation on these values. Then we proceed as we normally would to identify the optimal hedging strategy.[4]

SERIAL DEPENDENCE IN CURRENCY RETURNS

All of the results we have presented thus far presume that currency returns are random. This assumption may not be valid in light of recent evidence that suggests currency returns are positively serially correlated.[5]

Runs Test

One way to test for serial correlation is a runs test. A runs test is quite simple. For any time series, we compute the number of observations that are above the mean and the number of observations that are below the mean. In the case of currency returns, we are probably safe to assume that the population mean is close to zero so that we simply need to compare positive values to negative values. A *run* is an uninterrupted sequence of positive or negative values. Thus, if we were to observe four positive currency returns in a row (+ + + +), that would constitute a single run, whereas a sequence of four alternating values (+ − + −) would constitute four runs. For a series of returns that is distributed randomly, we can compute the expected number of runs and the standard deviation of runs based on the number of positive and negative values.[6] If there are significantly more runs than expected, the series follows a mean-reverting process and is negatively serially correlated (frequent reversals). If, instead, there are significantly fewer runs than expected, the series is characterized by trends and is positively serially correlated. In Table 7–2, we present the results of runs tests on five major currencies based on their monthly returns. The fact that the t-statistics are significantly negative, for the most part, indicates that there are significantly fewer (hence longer) runs than we would expect from a random series, supporting the view that currency returns follow trends.

Variance Ratio Test

We can also test for serial correlation with a test called a *variance ratio test*. This test is also quite simple. If returns are randomly distributed, then variances estimated from returns over differing time intervals should be related linearly. That is, a variance estimated from bimonthly returns

TABLE 7–2
Runs Test (January 1977–December 1988)

	Expected Number of Runs	Actual Number of Runs	t-Statistic
British pound	73	50	−3.84
German mark	72	57	−2.59
Japanese yen	73	66	−1.15
Swiss franc	73	57	−2.63
French franc	73	54	−2.93

should equal approximately twice the variance estimated from monthly returns, and a variance estimated from six-month returns should equal six times the variance estimated from monthly returns. The variance ratio itself is normalized by multiplying it by 1 over the number of months in the interval used to estimate the variance in the numerator. Thus, a value of less than 1 indicates that the returns are negatively serially correlated, while a value greater than 1 indicates that the returns are positively serially correlated, again implying that they follow trends. In Figure 7–4, we present the results of the variance ratio tests. The normalized variance ratios are greater than 1 for all of the currencies we tested, although they are not significant for ratios based on intervals of less than a year. As we extend the interval, though, the evidence strongly supports our view that

FIGURE 7–4
Variance Ratio Test (January 1977–December 1988)

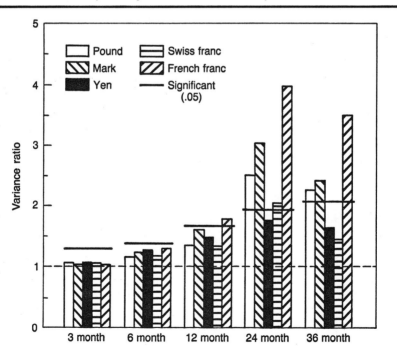

currency returns are serially dependent. The significance peaks at intervals around two years, suggesting that the trends tend to last about two years.[7]

What causes this apparent serial dependence? One possible explanation is that it is induced by central banks. Central banks, on balance, prefer stable exchange rates to volatile exchange rates, because stability promotes free trade. Thus, when there are disturbances in foreign exchange markets, they intervene to dampen the volatility. This intervention has the impact of protracting the movement to the new equilibrium exchange rate and dampening short-term volatility so that cyclical trends rise above the noise.

It may also be the case that frictions in moving capital across international borders contribute to serial dependence. To the extent that investors cannot act on their perceptions that exchange rates are in disequilibrium, exchange rates are less likely to be equilibrated quickly.

The investment implications of this serial dependence are both favorable and unfavorable. Since our strategies to minimize risk and construct optimal portfolios are based upon the assumption that investment returns are random, to the extent currency returns are not random, we may achieve suboptimal results. This outcome is unfavorable because in order to find the truly optimal solution, we must explicitly account for the serial dependence in currency returns, which is very complicated.[8]

The tradeoff is that serial dependence presents interesting investment opportunities. Recall from Chapter 4 that we can add value to a buy-and-hold strategy by following linear investment rules that generate convex payoff functions if we expect returns to follow trends. Since currency returns are positively serially correlated, they follow trends that we can exploit. We must be careful, however, about distinguishing results that are period specific from results that we believe will persist.

SUMMARY

- Diversification into foreign assets usually improves a portfolio's risk and return profile because foreign assets tend to have favorable diversification properties.
- The currency exposure that accompanies foreign investment, however, does not necessarily improve a portfolio's risk and return profile unless we expect the domestic currency to depreciate against foreign currencies or unless the foreign currencies have favorable hedging properties.

- We can determine the optimal currency exposure for our portfolio by measuring the sensitivity of our utility to currency exposure. If the sensitivity is positive, we increase exposure to the currency until the sensitivity equals zero. If the sensitivity is negative, we decrease exposure to the currency until the sensitivity equals zero.
- If we wish to protect the purchasing power of our portfolio and we consume foreign products, currency exposure may help to offset inflation that is induced by our consumption of foreign products. In this context, we can identify the minimum risk hedging strategy based upon estimates of expected return, standard deviation, and correlation from real returns.
- Empirical evidence suggests that currency returns are positively serially correlated. This serial dependence may result from central bank activity to stabilize exchange rates or from frictions that interfere with the movement of capital across international borders. Serial dependence violates some of the assumptions that underlie traditional optimization techniques; hence these optimization results may not be valid. However, given the presence of serial dependence, we may be able to add value to a portfolio that includes foreign assets by following a rule whereby we vary our currency exposure in accordance with an investment rule that generates a convex payoff function (see Chapter 4).

NOTES

1. In fact, the consensus expectation for the percentage change in the spot exchange rate equals the interest rate differential between the two countries, which in turn equals the forward premium or discount. Therefore, the consensus expectation for the return on a currency forward or futures contract equals 0 percent (expected change in spot rate less forward or futures contract). By defining currency return this way, we automatically subsume the dynamics of interest rate differentials in our estimates of inputs.
2. Consider a situation in which we expect a favorable return from a foreign asset in its local currency but we expect the foreign currency to depreciate against the domestic currency. We can benefit from the favorable expected return of the foreign asset by hedging away our currency risk. On the other hand, if we base our decision to invest in the foreign asset on its return denominated in the domestic currency, its composite return may not be sufficiently high to warrant

our investment, and we would unnecessarily forgo the favorable return of the foreign asset.

3. W. F. Sharpe, "An Algorithm for Portfolio Improvement" (Research Paper No. 475, Graduate School Business, Stanford University, October 1978).

4. Fischer Black has demonstrated that under certain assumptions, including the assumption that real returns are relevant, there is a universally optimal hedge ratio for currency exposure. For an elaboration of this notion, see F. Black, "Universal Hedging: How to Optimize Currency Risk and Reward in International Equity Portfolios," *Goldman Sachs Research Report*, March 1989.

5. For example, see M. Kritzman, "Serial Dependence in Currency Returns: Investment Implications," *The Journal of Portfolio Management* (Fall 1989).

6. We can compute the expected number of runs as:

$$\frac{2 \cdot n1 \cdot n2}{n1 + n2} + 1$$

and the standard deviation of runs as:

$$\frac{2 \cdot n1 \cdot n2 \, (2 \cdot n1 \cdot n2 - n1 - n2)}{(n1 - n2)^2 \cdot (n1 + n2 - 1)}$$

where

$n1$ = Number of positive observations

$n2$ = Number of negative observations

7. We can estimate the significance of a variance ratio based on overlapping returns as:

$$z(q) = n \cdot (VR - 1) \cdot (2 \, (2q - 1)(q - 1) / 3q)^{\frac{1}{2}}$$

where

$z(q)$ = Normal deviate

n = Number of observations used to estimate variance in denominator

VR = Normalized variance ratio

q = Number of periods in interval used to estimate variance in numerator

8. For a derivation of thissignificance formula and a more detailed discussion of variance ratios, see A. L. and A.C. MacKinlay, "Stock Market Prices Do Not Follow Random Walks: Evidence from a Simple Specification Test," *The Review of Financial Studies* 1, no. 1 (Spring 1988), pp. 41–66.

We can diminish the impact of serial dependence by revising our hedge ratio frequently.

AMERICAN FABRIC: PART 2

We rejoin Betsy Ross as she considers the potential impact of the new pension accounting rules on the asset mix she had just recommended to Tom Paine, President of American Fabric.

When we left Betsy Ross she had just decided to meet with Patrick Henry, her supervisor at American Fabric, to express her reservations about the asset allocation study she had just completed for Tom Paine, American Fabric's President.

"Patrick," said Betsy as she hesitantly entered his office. "May I speak with you for a moment?"

"Hello, Betsy. Have a seat. I understand you have become quite a star. Tom Paine told me how impressed he is with your asset allocation study. You should be very pleased with yourself."

"That's the problem," said Betsy. "I'm afraid that the conclusions of the study are incomplete, and that American Fabric may be exposed to more pension investment risk than Mr. Paine realizes."

"I don't understand, Betsy. Your study was extremely rigorous and it dealt explicitly with the pension liabilities."

"Patrick," said Betsy hesitantly, "I think I overlooked an important consideration."

"What do you mean?" asked Patrick in a tone that betrayed his growing concern.

"Patrick, as I understand it, the Financial Accounting Standards Board requires corporate pension fund sponsors to report a liability on the balance sheet if pension liabilities exceed pension assets. As a matter of fact, Mr. Paine cited this new rule as his primary reason in choosing the asset mix for the pension fund."

"That's right, Betsy, but I don't understand your concern. Your analysis focused on each strategy's likelihood of covering liabilities."

"That's true, Patrick, but one of the implicit assumptions of the analysis was that the liabilities would not fluctuate very much from year to year. My impression is that Mr. Paine focused on FASB's disclosure requirement but overlooked the new valuation rules. In any event, according to FASB, American Fabric has to value the liabilities in accordance with prevailing market interest rates. Since interest rates can change substantially from year to year, the present value of the liabilities may be as volatile or more volatile than stocks or bonds. I did not explicitly account for this volatility in my analysis, which is why I'm concerned about the inferences Mr. Paine has drawn from the analysis. For example, if interest rates fall, the value of the liabilities may increase more than the assets. The net result could be a liability that we would have to report on the balance sheet."

"I see your point, Betsy. You are exactly right about the accounting rules, and I know that Tom Paine would not be pleased to report a pension liability on the balance sheet. Is there some way you can modify the analysis to reflect fluctuations in the value of the liabilities?"

"I've thought about how to deal with this problem. In order to treat the liabilities stochastically, we need to estimate their return and standard deviation as well as their correlation with each of the asset classes. But I don't see how we can obtain the data that we need to estimate these values, since, historically, liabilities were valued according to unrealistic actuarial conventions."

"I have an idea, Betsy. What if I produce a historical record of the relevant cash flows under the new FASB rules? We can then look at past interest rates and value the liabilities as if we had been complying with the new rules all along."

"That would be great," exclaimed Betsy. "We can produce a time series of the liabilities, and from that information we can compute all of the return and risk statistics that we need to revise the analysis. Would you be able to provide me with the numbers, Patrick?"

"No problem, Betsy. We have just been assigned a summer intern from NYU. I'm sure he can come up with the information you need in a couple of days. I'll ask him to call you this afternoon so you can explain to him exactly what you are looking for. And I'll impress upon him our sense of urgency so as to expedite the process a little. You know how interns are always trying to impress their employer with their diligence. Keep me informed on your progress. When you are ready to see Tom Paine, let me know and we can approach him together."

After thanking Patrick profusely, Betsy returned to her office to contemplate precisely what she needed to do in order to recognize the stochastic nature of liabilities in her analysis. Her first thought was to add the liabilities to the efficient asset mixes she had already identified and to compute the expected return net of liabilities for each asset mix and the standard deviation of each mix net of liabilities. She knew that this approach would yield a more accurate estimate of the likelihood of experiencing a net liability on the balance sheet, but intuitively she felt troubled. Something just didn't seem right. Nonetheless, she decided to proceed along this course of action, at least as a preliminary step.

It was only two days before Betsy had a time series of liability returns. She had taken the quarterly values of the liabilities furnished to her by George, the summer intern, and she computed their percentage change each quarter for the past ten years. She then linked these numbers, calculated the geometric average, and annualized this value. Next, she computed the standard deviation of the quarterly returns and annualized this value by multiplying it by 2, since it is the square root of 4. She then regressed the liability returns against the quarterly returns for stocks, bonds, and short-term securities. Betsy wasn't surprised to find that the liabilities were more highly correlated with bonds and stocks than with short-term securities. She was surprised, however, by how volatile the liabilities were until she remembered how much interest rates had fluctuated in the late 70s and early 80s.

Liability return	4.5%
Liability standard deviation	14.5%
Liability correlations	
Stocks	51.3%
Bonds	89.8%
Short-term securities	−11.2%

Next, Betsy calculated the net expected return and net standard deviation for each of the efficient asset mixes she had identified in her earlier analysis based on the fact that the present value of the liabilities equaled 95 percent of the current asset value. In addition, she computed the likelihood that each mix had of funding the liabilities fully. She compared

Portfolio								
		1	*2*	*3*	*4*	*5*	*6*	*7*

Efficient Asset Mixes before Liabilities

Stock (percent)	2.4	10.3	20.2	30.1	42.9	71.4	100.0
Bond (percent)	2.2	15.2	31.5	47.8	57.1	28.6	0.0
Short-term (percent)	95.4	74.5	48.3	22.1	0.0	0.0	0.0

Gross of Liabilities

Expected return (percent)	7.2	8.0	9.0	10.0	11.0	12.0	13.0
Standard deviation (percent)	1.9	3.2	6.0	9.0	12.0	16.1	21.0

Net of Liabilities

Expected return (percent)	2.9	3.7	4.7	5.7	6.7	7.7	8.7
Standard deviation (percent)	13.7	11.7	9.5	8.0	8.1	12.9	18.3

Probability of Achieving Full Funding

Gross probability (percent)	99	99	99	95	91	85	80
Net probability (percent)	72	77	85	91	93	84	77

these net results to each portfolio's expected return and standard deviation gross of the liabilities.

As Betsy looked at these results, she noticed that the portfolio that Paine had selected from her original analysis did not offer the best chance of funding the liabilities, after accounting for the expected return and risk of the liabilities. Furthermore, as she examined the results more carefully, her earlier reservation about methodology resurfaced. She noticed that some of the portfolios were inefficient, when viewed in the context of net return and net risk. Indeed, the portfolios that included a large exposure to short-term securities had a lower net expected return and a higher net standard deviation than the portfolios with little or no short-term exposure. Moreover, the less risky "asset-only" portfolios were riskier when liabilities were treated explicitly while the risky "asset-only" portfolios appeared to be less risky. Initially, Betsy was perplexed, but soon her perplexity shifted to comprehension. "Of course," she thought to herself. "Not only do short-term securities have the lowest expected return, they don't hedge the liabilities. In fact, they are totally dominated by bonds and probably wouldn't appear in any portfolio along the efficient frontier when considered in the context of both assets and liabilities. I should redo the analysis by incorporating liabilities right from the start."

Betsy decided to proceed along this path by solving for the minimum "net" risk portfolio that had the same net expected return as the portfolios that she identified as efficient before including liabilities. In a couple of hours Betsy had modified her spreadsheet to incorporate the liabilities as a negative asset with a fixed allocation. Once she had completed this change, it took her less than 10 minutes to identify the new portfolios and to evaluate their probabilities of funding the liabilities.

Efficient Asset Mixes after Liabilities

Stock (percent)	16.0	42.9	71.4	100.0
Bond (percent)	84.0	57.1	28.6	0.0
Net expected return (percent)	5.8	6.7	7.7	8.7
Net standard deviation (percent)	5.8	8.1	12.9	18.3
Probability of full funding (percent)	97	93	84	78

As she expected, none of the efficient portfolios included any exposure to short-term securities. Betsy also noticed that the minimum net risk portfolio had a net expected return of 5.8 percent and a net standard deviation of 5.8 percent. Moreover, this portfolio had a 97 percent chance of funding the liabilities. She wasn't surprised to see that it was allocated 84 percent to bonds with the balance in stocks. She also noticed that she could raise the stock component to 43 percent and still expect to fund the liabilities with 93 percent confidence. She decided to share these results with Paine, but before she called his office for an appointment she went to visit Patrick.

Patrick was intrigued by Betsy's new analysis. As she explained the revised results and the implication for the short-term component of the portfolio, Patrick thought to himself, "Imagine trying to convince the Investment Committee that Treasury bills are risky. Somehow I think they might have trouble with that concept." His reverie was interrupted by Betsy's question.

"Patrick, do you think Mr. Paine will be upset? I'm worried that he might lose confidence in me. After all, it was only a few days ago that we recommended a different asset mix."

Patrick looked her straight in the eyes and said, "I honestly don't know Betsy. All I can say is that he has always been fair. At least we have not met with the Investment Committee yet. And you know that I'll lend whatever support I can. I admire your willingness to bring this issue up in the first place. There are a lot of people around this place who would not have the courage to do what you are doing. Many people in your position wouldn't take a chance with a new approach in the first place. They prefer to follow the crowd even when they are absolutely certain the crowd is wrong!"

Paine agreed to meet with Betsy the next afternoon.

"It's good to see you again, Betsy. How's our asset mix doing? Still efficient, I hope?"

For a brief moment Betsy thought of feigning illness and excusing herself, but she overcame the urge. "That's why I called to see you, Mr. Paine. After I left your office last week it occurred to me that the reasoning behind the decision to change the fund's allocation may have been flawed in light of the new pension accounting rules."

With that introduction Betsy and Patrick launched into a detailed explanation of FAS No. 87, focusing on the asset mix implications of these accounting changes.

"Do you mean to tell me that Treasury bills are riskier than bonds and possibly even stocks?" queried Paine with a somewhat puzzled expression.

"Yes, if our objective is to ensure that the pension fund will continue to have a surplus," responded Betsy and Patrick almost in unison. "Because the liabilities fluctuate inversely with changes in interest rates, bonds and even stocks are typically a better liability hedge than short-term securities."

Paine thought for a while and finally said, "Well, I guess from the perspective of both assets and liabilities and the short horizon that the accountants have forced upon us, your arguments make sense. I'll recommend to the Committee that we shift to a 43/57 mix between stocks and bonds as your revised analysis suggests, but I'd like you to explain the motivation for this change, Betsy."

Normally, Betsy would have been quite nervous about the prospect of facing such an unsympathetic group, but she knew that both Mr. Paine and Patrick would support her. Moreover, she was growing more and more confident in her position at American Fabric.

To be continued . . .

PART 3

PROCEDURAL ISSUES

CHAPTER 8

ESTIMATION ISSUES IN ASSET ALLOCATION

INTRODUCTION

Suppose we wish to identify the least risky combination of two assets, both of which have the same expected return, which we are able to estimate correctly. Suppose the assets are uncorrelated with each other and we also estimate this relationship correctly. Furthermore, suppose both assets have a standard deviation equal to 10 percent. What happens if we misestimate their standard deviations? For example, suppose we estimate one asset's standard deviation to equal 8 percent and the other asset's standard deviation to equal 12 percent. On average we are exactly right since these errors cancel each other out. However, it is the nature of optimization, whether we proceed formally or informally, to maximize our errors.[1] The minimum risk portfolio based upon our estimates is a 75 percent allocation to the asset we estimated to have the lower standard deviation and a 25 percent allocation to the asset we estimated to have the higher standard deviation. If we had estimated their standard deviations correctly, we would have discovered that the true minimum risk portfolio consists of an equal weighting between these two assets. Optimization emphasizes errors in our forecasts. Moreover, the problem worsens as we increase the number of candidate assets, because we increase the number of errors we are likely to make. The impact of estimation errors when we optimize is the opposite of choosing asset weights arbitrarily. If we arbitrarily allocate a portfolio across a set of assets, the net effect of our estimation error is reduced as we diversify across more assets. When we choose asset weights by optimization or, for that matter, any set of rules based on a comparison of expected return and risk, the effect is to magnify errors in our estimates of these values. On balance, optimization favors assets for which we have overestimated expected return or for which we have underestimated risk.

Since the success of an asset allocation strategy depends to a great degree on the reliability of our estimates, we should take care to ensure their accuracy.

THE PAST AS PROLOGUE[2]

Return

Historical precedent provides an excellent point of departure for estimating many of the values required for asset allocation strategies. Some historical values are more reliable than others, however. To the extent we wish to extrapolate historical data, we should be confident that the values we choose to extrapolate are reasonably stable through time or at least reflective of our investment horizon. In Table 8–1, we show the annualized 10-year returns from 1926 through 1988 for stocks, corporate bonds, and Treasury bills.

Even though these returns represent 10-year periods, they have varied quite substantially. In fact, if we shorten the measurement period, we find even greater disparity between the high and low returns. In Table 8–2, we show the highest and lowest returns for stocks, bonds, and Treasury bills for calendar year periods of 1, 5, and 10 years.

The obvious message from Table 8–2 is that the longer our investment horizon, the more confidence we should have in extrapolating historical results. Nonetheless, even with a 10-year investment horizon, the total returns for stocks, bonds, and Treasury bills have been significantly unstable.

As an alternative to extrapolating historical total returns, we may wish to extrapolate real returns and add to these values a forecast of the inflation premium. We may prefer this approach if we believe that historical real returns are more reliable than historical total returns.

Standard Deviation

Now let us consider the reliability of historical standard deviations. In Table 8–3, we show the historical standard deviations of stocks, bonds, and Treasury bills for every 10-year period from 1926 through 1988.

TABLE 8–1
Total Return (Annualized Percentage)

10 Years Ended	Common Stock	Corporate Bonds	Treasury Bills
1935	5.86	7.08	1.93
1936	7.81	7.02	1.63
1937	0.02	6.54	1.34
1938	−0.89	6.88	1.02
1939	−0.05	6.95	0.55
1940	1.80	6.49	0.32
1941	6.43	6.97	0.21
1942	9.35	6.15	0.15
1943	7.17	5.40	0.15
1944	9.28	4.53	0.17
1945	8.42	3.99	0.18
1946	4.41	3.49	0.20
1947	9.62	2.96	0.22
1948	7.26	2.77	0.30
1949	9.17	2.70	0.41
1950	13.38	2.57	0.53
1951	17.28	2.02	0.67
1952	17.09	2.11	0.81
1953	14.31	2.17	0.96
1954	17.21	2.23	1.01
1955	16.69	1.87	1.14
1956	18.43	0.98	1.35
1957	16.44	2.07	1.67
1958	20.06	1.43	1.68
1959	19.35	1.00	1.87
1960	16.16	1.67	2.01
1961	16.43	2.43	2.08
1962	13.44	2.86	2.19
1963	15.91	2.74	2.31
1964	12.82	2.68	2.58
1965	11.06	2.58	2.82
1966	9.20	3.33	3.05
1967	12.85	1.95	3.15
1968	10.00	2.44	3.52
1969	7.81	1.68	3.88
1970	8.18	2.51	4.26
1971	7.06	3.10	4.49
1972	9.93	3.04	4.60
1973	6.00	2.93	4.98
1974	1.24	2.13	5.43
1975	3.27	3.59	5.62

TABLE 8–1 *Concluded*

10 Years Ended	Common Stock	Corporate Bonds	Treasury Bills
1976	6.63	5.35	5.65
1977	3.59	6.07	5.74
1978	3.16	5.79	5.94
1979	5.86	6.23	6.31
1980	8.44	4.18	6.77
1981	6.47	3.00	7.78
1982	6.68	6.06	8.46
1983	10.61	6.43	8.65
1984	14.76	8.39	8.83
1985	14.33	9.84	9.03
1986	13.85	9.84	9.11
1987	15.26	9.70	9.20
1988	16.30	10.91	9.17

TABLE 8–2
Highest and Lowest Total Returns: 1926–1988 (Annualized Percentage)

	1 Year	5 Years	10 Years
Common stock			
High	53.99	23.92	20.06
Low	−43.34	−12.47	−0.89
Corporate bonds			
High	43.79	22.16	10.91
Low	−8.09	−2.22	0.98
Treasury bills			
High	14.71	11.12	9.20
Low	−0.02	0.07	0.15

TABLE 8–3
Standard Deviation (Annualized Percentage)

10 Years Ended	Common Stock	Corporate Bonds	Treasury Bills
1935	35.35	4.72	0.50
1936	35.37	4.73	0.59
1937	36.08	4.76	0.49
1938	37.79	4.76	0.43
1939	37.67	4.96	0.25
1940	37.60	4.96	0.15
1941	35.12	4.59	0.13
1942	28.80	4.08	0.06
1943	23.40	2.49	0.05
1944	22.53	2.26	0.05
1945	22.25	2.13	0.05
1946	22.50	2.19	0.05
1947	21.09	2.27	0.06
1948	17.90	2.24	0.08
1949	15.83	1.73	0.10
1950	13.98	1.65	0.11
1951	13.59	2.04	0.13
1952	13.29	2.20	0.15
1953	12.80	2.72	0.16
1954	13.42	2.78	0.16
1955	13.33	2.82	0.15
1956	12.71	3.02	0.17
1957	13.15	3.98	0.21
1958	11.93	4.18	0.21
1959	11.79	4.30	0.23
1960	12.08	4.48	0.25
1961	11.82	4.42	0.24
1962	13.00	4.41	0.24
1963	12.97	4.12	0.25
1964	12.13	4.09	0.23
1965	11.72	4.08	0.23
1966	11.48	4.13	0.28
1967	11.30	3.96	0.30
1968	11.59	4.28	0.29
1969	12.10	4.78	0.38
1970	12.93	5.62	0.41
1971	13.23	6.35	0.37
1972	11.86	6.38	0.34
1973	12.35	6.76	0.37
1974	14.54	7.63	0.43
1975	15.52	8.25	0.41
1976	15.73	8.30	0.41
1977	15.54	8.04	0.39

TABLE 8–3 *Concluded*

10 Years Ended	Common Stock	Corporate Bonds	Treasury Bills
1978	15.84	7.86	0.41
1979	15.86	8.15	0.55
1980	15.76	9.84	0.73
1981	15.74	11.25	0.93
1982	16.67	12.20	0.90
1983	16.29	12.45	0.88
1984	14.74	12.54	0.89
1985	14.15	12.70	0.85
1986	14.55	12.88	0.82
1987	16.87	13.02	0.79
1988	16.38	13.01	0.80

In Table 8–4, we show the high and low values for standard deviation.

It is clear from Table 8–4 that standard deviations have also varied quite extensively since 1926. As we might expect, though, some of the variability is diversified away when we extend the measurement interval.

Correlation

Finally, let us examine historical correlations. In Table 8–5, we show the correlations between stocks and bonds, stocks and Treasury bills, and bonds and Treasury bills for every 10-year period from 1926 through 1988.

As you might expect by now, in Table 8–6 we show the high and low values for historical correlations.

As with returns and standard deviations, correlations are more stable for longer measurement periods than they are for shorter measurement periods, although the values have also varied quite substantially through time. The bad news for correlation is that, short of pure judgment, historical extrapolation is the only method available to us for estimating correlations. The good news, however, is that errors in our estimates of correlation are typically less damaging than errors in our estimates of return and standard deviation.

TABLE 8–4
Highest and Lowest Standard Deviations: 1926 –1988 (Annualized Percentage)

	1 Year	5 Years	10 Years
Common stock			
High	65.12	46.72	37.79
Low	3.85	9.70	11.30
Corporate bonds			
High	19.91	16.02	13.02
Low	0.68	1.19	1.65
Treasury bills			
High	0.85	1.00	0.93
Low	0.00	0.02	0.05

AN ALTERNATIVE APPROACH FOR ESTIMATING RETURN

Although historical precedent may be useful for establishing a frame of reference in which to estimate return, we would not be prudent to rely exclusively on historical data, especially in light of its variability. As an alternative to extrapolation, we may wish to apply a more prospective approach to estimate return. For example, we can estimate future cash flows based upon fundamental considerations and solve for the internal rate of return that equates these cash flows with present value. We presented a single-year model of this approach in our discussion of tactical asset allocation. We will now present this approach assuming we have a five-year investment horizon.

In order to estimate the return for stocks, we need to forecast a dividend payout ratio, a growth rate for earnings, and an equilibrium price/earnings multiple.

The dividend payout ratio is fairly stable, especially for a large sample of companies, so we are probably fairly safe to extrapolate historical data. We may wish to superimpose our subjective views, however,

TABLE 8–5
Correlation (Percentage)

10 Years Ended	Common Stock/ Corporate Bonds	Common Stock/ Treasury Bills	Corporate Bonds/ Treasury Bills
1935	17.62	−0.48	−14.35
1936	17.81	−1.48	−14.63
1937	17.60	−0.55	−13.03
1938	20.97	−6.54	−9.57
1939	22.89	−6.93	−4.43
1940	23.95	−1.93	−10.92
1941	25.26	6.57	0.31
1942	24.37	43.69	21.60
1943	28.30	19.37	13.75
1944	29.42	17.39	7.13
1945	30.34	19.58	6.95
1946	32.91	17.07	4.30
1947	37.11	19.26	−12.35
1948	27.77	18.80	−7.83
1949	23.76	15.98	−6.31
1950	18.86	15.30	−6.77
1951	25.49	8.80	−16.18
1952	27.87	6.82	−9.81
1953	28.54	−0.10	−5.22
1954	26.76	0.69	−2.19
1955	23.43	5.70	1.99
1956	15.61	−8.33	−12.13
1957	0.31	−23.44	0.43
1958	−1.83	−28.08	7.72
1959	−0.60	−28.49	6.54
1960	−2.35	−30.36	12.30
1961	−5.94	−31.22	9.63
1962	−8.56	−30.61	12.08
1963	−14.27	−28.00	12.45
1964	−15.57	−19.74	18.62
1965	−13.20	−14.69	11.06
1966	−2.21	−21.29	3.13
1967	21.43	−16.04	1.26
1968	16.36	−6.59	−5.30
1969	20.89	−12.97	−17.27
1970	36.51	−13.73	0.47
1971	35.62	−8.65	6.63
1972	42.45	−17.84	9.85
1973	35.99	−17.48	8.62
1974	44.00	−28.85	0.90
1975	47.42	−24.10	3.51

TABLE 8–5 *Concluded*

10 Years Ended	Common Stock/ Corporate Bonds	Common Stock/ Treasury Bills	Corporate Bonds/ Treasury Bills
1976	46.34	−25.79	0.77
1977	46.41	−22.99	−3.95
1978	51.34	−20.81	−7.81
1979	53.00	−10.17	−12.62
1980	35.26	−6.17	1.08
1981	37.96	−8.87	0.50
1982	40.83	−8.64	−4.58
1983	45.18	−12.48	3.31
1984	39.32	−12.39	6.08
1985	39.83	−10.64	5.51
1986	41.14	−9.48	5.99
1987	32.19	−14.57	5.67
1988	32.98	−16.05	4.75

TABLE 8–6
Highest and Lowest Correlations (Percentage): 1926–1988

	1 Year	5 Years	10 Years
Common stock corporate bonds			
High	79.67	61.02	53.00
Low	−46.67	−24.43	−15.57
Common stock/ Treasury bills			
High	88.61	54.14	43.69
Low	−68.65	−40.74	−31.22
Corporate bonds/ Treasury bills			
High	73.73	26.16	21.60
Low	−63.03	−46.37	−17.27

if we feel it is appropriate to do so. For example, if we expect earnings to grow sharply, we may wish to lower the historical payout ratio, whereas if we expect earnings to fall sharply, we may choose to raise the payout ratio. The rationale for these adjustments is that companies manage dividends so that they tend to be less volatile than earnings.

Unless we have a particularly strong conviction about earnings growth, we are probably safe to base our estimate on the market consensus forecast. There are services that collect and tabulate these forecasts from the major research organizations. Quite often the consensus forecast will differ depending on whether it is based upon a direct forecast for the total market or the sum of forecasts for individual companies. Typically, the market-based forecast will be lower than the company-based forecast, because research analysts have a tendency to be optimistic about the individual companies they follow. Thus, we would be more conservative to use the market-based forecast of earnings growth.

Finally, we need to estimate an equilibrium value for the market's price/earnings multiple. Again, we may wish to start with historical values and adjust them based upon fundamental considerations. For example, we may wish to use the historical average as a point of departure and adjust it according to our expectations about return on equity, interest rates, and the relative risk of stocks and bonds. On balance, our estimate for the equilibrium price/earnings multiple should be positively related to return on equity, negatively related to our expectation for interest rates, and negatively related to the risk premium of stocks over bonds. Moreover, in evaluating this risk premium, we may wish to consider such factors as the impact of increased leverage to finance corporate takeovers on the stock market's riskiness.

We have just mentioned a representative sample of the types of considerations that may influence our estimate of return for stocks. Admittedly, there are many other factors that we could consider, including economic and political factors as well as imponderables such as investor sentiment.

Suppose that our index for the stock market currently equals $100 and that the prior year's earnings were $9. Furthermore, suppose that after careful consideration and research we estimate that the dividend payout ratio will remain constant at 40 percent, earnings will grow at an annual rate of 10 percent, and the stock market's price/earnings multiple will move to an equilibrium value of 12 in five years. With these assumptions we can easily infer the expected return for the stock market. We simply need to discount the cash flows implicit in our assumptions back to the stock market's current price, using Formula 8–1.

Formula 8–1   Internal Rate of Return for Stocks

$$P = \frac{E \cdot (1 + g) \cdot p}{(1 + r)} + \frac{E \cdot (1 + g)^2 \cdot p}{(1 + r)^2} + \frac{E \cdot (1 + g)^3 \cdot p}{(1 + r)^3}$$

$$+ \frac{E \cdot (1 + g)^4 \cdot p}{(1 + r)^4} + \frac{(E \cdot p + E \cdot PE) \cdot (1 + g)^5}{(1 + r)^5}$$

where

P = Current price

E = Last year's earnings

g = Growth rate of earnings

p = Dividend payout ratio

PE = Equilibrium price/earnings multiple

r = Internal rate of return

Now let us substitute our assumptions as shown below into Formula 8–1.

Current price:	$100
Last year's earnings:	$ 9
Growth rate of earnings:	10%
Dividend payout ratio:	40%
Equilibrium price/earnings multiple:	12

$$100 = \frac{9 \cdot (1.1) \cdot .4}{(1 + r)} + \frac{9 \cdot (1.1)^2 \cdot .4}{(1 + r)^2} + \frac{9 \cdot (1.1)^3 \cdot .4}{(1 + r)^3}$$

$$+ \frac{9 \cdot (1.1)^4 \cdot .4}{(1 + r)^4} + \frac{(9 \cdot .4 + 9 \cdot 12) \cdot (1.1)^5}{(1 + r)^5} \quad r = .1555$$

We cannot solve directly for r, the internal rate of return. Instead, we must substitute various values for r until the sum of the values of the discounted cash flows equal $100. Most spreadsheet software includes functions that perform this trial and error task automatically, as do some calculators. Also, in Appendix D, we present a numerical procedure for solving these types of problems quickly. However we proceed, we will eventually discover that the internal rate of return that discounts the cash flows to $100 equals 15.55 percent, which, of course, is synonymous with our expected return for stocks.

We can apply the same logic to estimate bond return. In fact, we need only estimte one unknown value, the equilibrium yield to maturity at the end of our investment horizon. With an estimate of this value, together with known values for face amount, coupon payments, and term to maturity, we can use Formula 8–2 to estimate a bond's return.

Formula 8–2   Internal Rate of Return for Bonds

$$P = \frac{C}{(1 + r)} + \frac{C}{(1 + r)^2} + \frac{C}{(1 + r)^3} + \frac{C}{(1 + r)^4}$$

$$+ \frac{C + C/i + (F - C/i)/(1 + i)^n}{(1 + r)^5}$$

where

P = Current bond price

C = Annual coupon payment

i = Equilibrium yield to maturity

F = Face value

n = Number of years to maturity at end of horizon

r = Internal rate of return

As with our stock example, we find the internal rate of return through a process of trial and error. Suppose that current price equals $100, the annual coupon equals $8, we estimate the equilibrium yield to maturity as 9 percent, the face value equals $100, and the number of years remaining to maturity at the end of the investment horizon equals 10. If we insert these values into Formula 8–2 and try various values for r, we will eventually find that the internal rate of return equals 6.88 percent, as shown below.

Current price:	$100
Annual coupon payment:	$ 8
Equilibrium yield to maturity:	9%
Face value:	$100
Number of years to maturity at end of horizon:	10

$$100 = \frac{8}{(1+r)} + \frac{8}{(1+r)^2} + \frac{8}{(1+r)^3} + \frac{8}{(1+r)^4}$$

$$+ \; \frac{8 + 8/.09 + (100 - 8/.09)/(1.09)^{10}}{(1+r)^5}$$

$$r = .0688$$

AN ALTERNATIVE APPROACH FOR ESTIMATING STANDARD DEVIATION

In our discussion of dynamic hedging strategies in Chapter 3, we reviewed the valuation of options. We showed that the value of an option is a function of five variables: the price of the underlying risky asset, the strike price, the riskless rate of interest, the time remaining to expiration, and the standard deviation of the underlying risky asset. We can observe all of these variables except standard deviation simply by reading the newspaper. Moreover, we can observe the prices at which options trade. Therefore, since we can observe all of the relevant values except standard deviation, we can substitute various estimates for standard deviation into the option pricing formula until one of these estimates yields the precise price at which the option traded. This estimate of standard deviation represents the consensus expectation of participants in the option market, and it is called *implied volatility*.

Remember from Chapter 2 that the value of a call option can be determined as shown in Formula 8–3.

Formula 8–3 Value of a Call Option

$$C = R \cdot N(D) - Ke^{-rT} \cdot N(D - S \cdot \sqrt{T})$$

$$D = \frac{ln\,(R/K) + r + S^2/2) \cdot T}{S \cdot \sqrt{T}}$$

where

C = Value of call option

R = Value of risky asset

K = Strike price

r = Riskless rate of interest

S = Standard deviation of risky asset

T = Time remaining to expiration

$N(\ )$ = Cumulative normal density function

ln = Natural log

e = 2.7128 (constant)

Suppose we look in the paper and observe that a call option on the Standard & Poor's 500 Stock Average that has a strike price of $275 and is due to expire in 90 days traded for $12. Suppose that the index was valued at $290 at the time of the trade and that the rate of interest on a riskless instrument due to mature in 90 days was 8 percent. How do we determine the standard deviation that corresponds to the option's price? As with the internal rate of return, we must substitute different values for the standard deviation of the underlying asset until one of our guesses yields a price of $12. Suppose we start with an estimate of 20 percent. If we substitute this value into the Black-Scholes equation along with the other values we observed, the fair price of the option equals $9. Since this value is lower than the actual value at which the option traded, we try a higher estimate for standard deviation on our next try. Suppose we try a value of 30 percent. (We raise our estimate because the value of an option is positively related to the volatility of the underlying asset.[3]) This estimate yields an option value of $15, which is too high. Thus, we try 25 percent, a value in between. Eventually, we will discover that the standard deviation consistent with the price at which the option traded equals 22.36 percent. In order to prevent "eventually" from reaching several weeks, we should follow a procedure that minimizes the number of trials. Again, in Appendix D, we present a search procedure that usually converges to a solution in two or three trials.

When we estimate implied volatility, we should take care to ensure that we use contemporaneous observations for the option price and the asset price or our estimate could be substantially incorrect. We are fairly safe if we choose the closing values for a liquid option that is close to the money and not too close to expiration. Options that are close to the money tend to be relatively liquid. The problem with using options that are about to expire is that it may not be prudent to assume that the distribution of the underlying asset's return is log normal, which is an assumption of the Black-Scholes formula.

SUMMARY

- The success of asset allocation strategies depends greatly on the precision with which we estimate the required inputs. In fact, in many applications, errors in our inputs are maximized rather than diversified away.
- Historical precedent provides a reasonable point of departure, but we may wish to adjust estimates derived from historical data to reflect prevailing economic and capital market conditions.
- Moreover, we should have a good understanding of the reliability of historical data, since some variables are significantly more stable than others.
- As an alternative to historical extrapolation, we can employ discounted cash flow models to estimate asset class returns, and we can infer standard deviations from the price of index options.

NOTES

1. For an excellent discussion of the sensitivity of optimization results to estimation error, see R. Michaud, "The Markowitz Optimization Enigma: Is 'Optimized' Optimal?" *Financial Analysts Journal* (January/February 1989), pp. 31–42.

2. All of the statistics in Tables 8–1 through 8–6 are estimated from data included in R. Ibbotson and R. Sinquefield, *Stocks, Bonds, Bills and Inflation: The Past and the Future 1988 Edition*, (The Financial Analysts Research Foundation, 1989).

3. The derivative of price with respect to volatility equals:

$$\delta P/\delta S = S \cdot \sqrt{T} \cdot (1/\sqrt{2\pi})e - x^2/2$$

where

P = Option price
S = Standard deviation of underlying asset
K = Strike price
r = Riskless rate of interest
T = Time remaining to expiration

and

$$X = ln\ (S/Kr^{-rT}) + 1/2 \cdot S \cdot \sqrt{T}$$

CHAPTER 9

EXECUTION OF ASSET ALLOCATION DECISIONS

"The real world is an uninteresting special case of my model."

Academic Proverb

INTRODUCTION

Imagine that we are responsible for the asset allocation of a $100 million pension fund. Currently, 60 percent of the fund is allocated to stocks and 40 percent is allocated to bonds. We wish to reduce the stock exposure to 50 percent and raise the bond exposure to 50 percent. The stock position is allocated among three equity managers, each of whom has a unique style. Similarly, the bond position is allocated between two managers with different styles. We are pleased with the performance of our managers and expect them all to add value to their respective benchmarks. How should we proceed? We might consider transferring an equal share from each equity manager and allocating it equally to our two fixed-income managers. Or we might try to distinguish among the expected performance of our managers and reallocate the fund based on expected performance. Both of these approaches involve the transfer of capital, which can be quite expensive. First of all, the affected equity managers must sell securities incurring commission costs and market impact costs.[1] The affected bond managers also incur transaction costs as they invest the cash in the bond market. There are also significant administrative costs involved in buying and selling securities, since financial institutions that serve as trustees or custodians typically base their fees on the number of transactions in a period. Assuming our decision to reallocate the fund was motivated by our view of the broad equity and bond markets, we will also sacrifice the premium we expect our managers to achieve relative to the market averages. Finally, these transactions are disruptive to investment managers and may actually impair their performance. All in all, the associated costs of reallocating a fund by transferring assets among investment managers impose a significant hurdle for asset allocation.

Fortunately, we can achieve our intended exposure to stocks and bonds without any disruption to our managers whatsoever, and in fact, even without their involvement or knowledge. We can sell stock index futures to reduce our exposure to the stock market and purchase bond futures to increase our exposure to the bond market. These transactions do not require the transfer of capital,[2] and they are relatively inexpensive to execute.

FINANCIAL FUTURES

A financial *futures contract* obligates a seller to pay the value of the futures contract to the buyer at a specified date. Since financial futures contracts typically have uniform terms with respect to quantity, expiration date, and underlying asset, there is a vast, well-organized secondary market.

The fair value of a financial futures contract is based on the principle of *arbitrage*. Suppose that we can purchase a financial asset valued at $300 on margin and that our interest cost is $6 for three months. Suppose that at the end of this period, the financial asset appreciates to $320, at which point we sell it. Our total profit from this transaction equals $14 ($320 − $300 − $6). Now suppose that, instead of purchasing the financial asset on margin, we can purchase a futures contract on this asset that expires in three months. The fair value of this contract should be the price that yields a $14 profit if we hold this futures contract to expiration. Since we can exchange the contract for the underlying asset at expiration, its value at expiration must equal $320. Thus, a purchase price of $306 yields a $14 profit ($320 − $306). If the futures contract sold for less than $306, we could buy the futures contract and sell the underlying asset short, thereby earning a riskless profit. If, on the other hand, the futures contract sold for more than $306, we could buy the underlying asset and sell the futures contract, again earning a riskless profit. Arbitrageurs monitor the relationship between the prices of financial futures and their underlying assets and engage in arbitrage transactions whenever the opportunity exists. This activity prevents futures prices from moving significantly away from their fair values. The range of values around fair value is determined by the ease at which arbitrageurs can profit from a misvalued futures contract. For example, to hedge a financial futures contract that is based on a stock index, we must buy or sell the entire index or a group of securities that tracks the index closely. This transaction can be very expensive if some of the component securities are not sufficiently liquid. In this case, transaction costs may offset the gain from the misvaluation, so that arbitrage is not profitable. In general, the more expensive or uncertain it is to transact in the underlying asset, the further away from fair value the contract price is likely to move before arbitrageurs enter the market.

The interest cost associated with purchasing the underlying asset on margin is called the *cost of carry* which, in our example, equals $6. In many cases, financial assets produce income. If we purchase the asset on margin, we are entitled to any income it produces. Suppose the asset in our example produces $3 in income, which is paid to us the day we sell it. In this case our profit from the transaction equals $17 instead of $14. However, if we purchase a futures contract on an asset, we must forgo any income the asset generates. Thus, based on the same arbitrage arguments, the fair value of a futures contract on this asset (now assuming it pays $3 in income) equals $303 instead of our original estimate of $306, as shown below.

	Underlying Asset	Futures Contract
Beginning price	$300	$303
Interest cost	6	0
Dividend	3	0
Ending price	320	320
Profit	$ 17	$ 17

Within this context, we can define our *net cost of carry* as the interest expense associated with purchasing the àsset on margin less the income we forgo when we purchase the futures contract which, in our example, equals $3 ($6 − $3). We can compute the fair value of a financial futures contract as shown in Formula 9–1.

Formula 9–1   Fair Value of Financial Futures Contract

$$F = P + C$$

where

F = Fair value of financial futures contract

P = Current price of underlying asset

C = Net carrying costs through expiration of contract (interest cost – income)

We can see from Formula 9–1 that in order to compute the fair value of a futures contract precisely, we must know the exact amount and incidence of the cash flows that represent the income attributable to the underlying asset. For stocks, we cannot always anticipate dividend payments exactly. To the extent we misestimate dividend payments, our estimate of the futures contract's fair value will be inexact.

Obviously, coupon payments are more reliable than dividend payments, so we need not worry too much about estimating income for bonds. We must deal with another complexity, though. The Treasury bond futures contract is based on a 20-year bond with a coupon yield of 8 percent. However, we can deliver any Treasury bond with a minimum of 15 years to maturity or first call. Thus, we must compute a *delivery factor*[3] for all deliverable bonds to determine which bond is cheapest to deliver (lowest corresponding futures value). We can adjust Formula 9–1 by the delivery factor, as shown in Formula 9–2.[4]

Formula 9–2   Fair Value of Financial Futures Contract Adjusted for Delivery Factor

$$F = P/D + C/D$$

where

F = Fair value of futures contract

P = Price of underlying asset

C = Net carrying costs through expiration of contract

D = Delivery factor

A STRAIGHTFORWARD EXAMPLE USING
FINANCIAL FUTURES

Let us return to our earlier example where we wish to change the allocation of our fund from a mix of 60 percent stocks and 40 percent bonds to a mix of 50 percent stocks and 50 percent bonds. However, let us assume that our $100 million fund is not managed by three equity managers and two fixed-income managers. Rather, we will assume that the equity component is allocated to a Standard & Poor's 500 index fund while the bond component is allocated to a 20-year Treasury bond with a coupon yield of 8 percent. How can we go about reducing the equity component by $10 million and increasing the bond component by an equal amount, assuming we transact only in the futures market? Suppose that the Standard & Poor's 500 average is currently valued at $300, while the contract size for a Treasury bond futures contracts is $100,000. The relevant information is summarized below:

Fund assets:	$100 million
Stock component:	S&P 500 Index Fund
Bond component:	20-year Treasury bond with 8% coupon yield
Current asset mix:	60% stocks, 40% bonds
Target asset mix:	50% stocks, 50% bonds
S&P 500 price:	$300.00
S&P 500 contract size:	500 times index price
Treasury bond contract size:	$100,000

In Table 9–1, we show the transactions necessary to reduce our fund's equity exposure by $10 million and increase its bond exposure by an equal amount.

As we can see from Table 9–1, we need not disrupt the underlying portfolio. We can achieve the desired exposure to stocks and bonds merely by buying and selling financial futures contracts.

A MORE REALISTIC (COMPLICATED) EXAMPLE
USING FINANCIAL FUTURES

The previous example was indeed straightforward, but unfortunately, not very realistic. Most funds are typically invested in portfolios that are

TABLE 9–1
Shifting from 60/40 to 50/50 Using Financial Futures

	Stocks	Bonds
Starting Position:		
Underlying asset	60,000,000	40,000,000
Futures position	0	0
Net exposure	60,000,000	40,000,000
Transactions:		
	Sell 67 S&P	Buy 100 T-bond
	500 contracts	contracts
	300.00 · 500	
	= 150,000	
	150,000 · − 67	100,000 · 100
	= −10,000,000	= 10,000,000
Ending Position:		
Underlying asset	60,000,000	40,000,000
Futures position	−10,000,000	10,000,000
Net exposure	50,000,000	50,000,000

managed actively and thus differ from the Standard & Poor's 500 Stock Average and 20-year Treasury bonds. They differ in two ways. First, they are more or less exposed to systematic sources of risk. Second, they are exposed to specific sources of risk. We should control for systematic risk since it is not a discretionary active management decision, but rather a reflection of our appetite for risk. On the other hand, managers expose a fund to specific sources of risk in an effort to generate above-average returns. If we control for specific risk, we eliminate the opportunity to achieve excess return. Thus, we should not control for specific risk.

We can estimate systematic risk for equity portfolios by regressing the portfolio's return against the overall market's return.[5] The slope of the regression line is called *beta*, and it represents the sensitivity of our fund's return to the market's return. For example, if our fund's *beta* equals 1.10 and the market returns 10 percent, we would expect our fund to return 11 percent. If the market returns −10 percent, we would expect our fund to return −11 percent. The extent to which its actual return is above or below 11 percent can be attributed to the discretionary management of the fund. A *beta* greater than 1 implies that our fund has greater exposure to systematic sources of risk than the overall market, whereas a *beta* of less than 1 implies the opposite. By convention, we relate systematic risk to moves in the broad market portfolio because these moves are deemed to be caused by economic, political, and social forces which cannot be diversified away. Company-specific sources of risk are diversified away and hence do not affect the broad market portfolio. Also, by convention, the broad market portfolio is usually defined as Standard & Poor's 500 Stock Average.

We can adjust the number of futures contracts we need to trade in order to account for our equity component's systematic risk as shown in Formula 9–3.

Formula 9–3   Beta Adjustment

$$N = \frac{T}{S} \cdot \beta$$

where

N = Number of contracts

T = Transaction amount

S = Size of contract

β = *Beta* of portfolio equity component

Thus, if we wish to reduce the equity exposure of our $100 million fund by 10 percent, and our equity component's *beta* equals 1.08, rather than sell 67 S&P 500 contracts, we should sell 72 contracts, as shown below.

$$-72 = \frac{-10,000,000}{150,000} \cdot 1.08$$

For bonds, systematic risk is measured by a bond's sensitivity to changes in the level of interest rates. This measure is called *duration*, and it equals the average time to receipt of a bond's cash flows weighted by their present values. Interestingly, but not surprisingly, duration is equivalent to the derivative of price with respect to a change in interest rates. For example, if a bond's duration equals 5 and interest rates increase by 1 percentage point, the price of the bond will decline by 5 percent. Alternatively, if interest rates fall by 1 percentage point, the price of a bond with a duration of 5 will increase by 5 percent. Duration differs from term to maturity in two ways. Term to maturity measures the time remaining to the final principal repayment, whereas duration measures the average time remaining to receipt of all the cash flows—coupon payments as well as interim principal repayments. Moreover, duration is weighted by the present value of the cash flows.

We can adjust the number of futures contracts we need to trade in order to account for our bond component's systematic risk, as shown in Formula 9–4.

Formula 9–4   Duration Adjustment

$$N = \frac{T}{S} \cdot \frac{D_P}{D_F}$$

where

N = Number of contracts
T = Transaction amount
S = Size of contract
D_P = Duration of portfolio bond component
D_F = Duration of Treasury bond that underlies futures contract

Based on Formula 9–4, if we wish to increase the bond component of our $100 million fund by 10 percent, assuming its duration equals 12 and the duration of the Treasury bond that underlies the futures contract equals 10, we should purchase 120 contracts instead of 100 contracts, as shown below:

$$120 = \frac{10,000,000}{100,000} \cdot \frac{12}{10}$$

In our preceding example, we assumed that our equity component and our bond component are both riskier than the respective futures contracts that we used as proxies. Thus we adjusted the magnitude of the futures transactions in order to achieve the same level of systematic risk as the equity and bonds components of our underlying portfolio.

Suppose that we are correct in anticipating the relative performance of stocks and bonds. (Implicit in our asset allocation decision is the

TABLE 9–2
Transaction Strategies

	Stocks B = 1.08	S&P 500 Futures	Bonds D = 12	T-Bond D = 10	Market Value
S&P 500 Return:	−3 percent				
20-Year T-Bond Yield Change:	−1 percentage point				
Transfer assets					
Exposure	50.00	0.00	50.00	0.00	100.00
Profit/loss	−1.62	0.00	6.00	0.00	4.38

Use futures,
  Ignore beta
  and duration					

Exposure	60.00	−10.00	40.00	10.00	100.00
Profit/loss	−1.94	.30	4.80	1.00	4.16

Use futures,
  Adjust for beta
  and duration					

Exposure	60.00	−10.80	40.00	12.00	100.00
Profit/loss	−1.94	.32	4.80	1.20	4.38

expectation that bonds will outperform stocks.) Suppose that the interest rate on the 20-year Treasury bond falls by one percentage point while the S&P 500 declines 3 percent. In Table 9–2, we show the change in value of our fund under three assumptions: (1) that we actually transferred the assets from our stock portfolio to our bond portfolio; (2) that we ignored our fund's *beta* and relative duration and traded futures in amounts equal to $10 million; and (3) that we factored in our fund's *beta* and relative duration in determining the number of futures contracts to trade.

It is clear from Table 9–2 that unless we adjust our futures positions to account for the systematic risk of our portfolio, we will not achieve the same outcome as we would by actually transferring the assets.

INSTITUTIONAL CONSIDERATIONS IN USING FINANCIAL FUTURES

In theory, it is fairly simple to execute asset allocation decisions with financial futures. In practice, however, there are important institutional considerations that we cannot ignore. Since we purchase the futures contracts with borrowed funds, we must deposit a specified amount of margin. There are two kinds of margin: initial margin and variation margin.

Initial margin is an amount we must deposit with a broker to commence a transaction. The amount changes from time to time and typically differs depending on whether we are trading the futures to speculate or to hedge. As of March 31, 1989, the initial margin requirement for hedgers for an S&P 500 contract was $4,000, which at the time was less than 3 percent of the contract's value. The initial margin requirement for speculators was $20,000 per contract, reflecting the additional risk associated with speculation. As of March 31, 1989, the initial margin requirement for hedgers for a 20-year Treasury bond contract was $2,000, which also was less than 3 percent of the contract's value. The initial margin requirement for speculators was $2,500.

As the value of the underlying asset changes, margin requirements change accordingly. Margin that is required to cover variation in the underlying asset's value appropriately is called *variation margin*. Futures exchanges require that we settle variation margin requirements the business day after the market closes. Thus, funds must be wired back and forth between our bank and our broker's bank to settle variation margin requirements. This requirement can impose a significant administrative hardship on investors who choose to execute asset allocation decisions with financial futures.

When we use futures we also face a decision about when to roll over our futures position into the next contract. For example, suppose we are currently long 75 S&P 500 March futures contracts. As the expiration date approaches, we must roll over this position into June or later contracts, or our chosen asset mix will change. If we wait until the actual expiration date, we may be forced to purchase June contracts that are overpriced. Moreover, distant contracts are not often sufficiently liquid to absorb a substantial transaction without affecting the price. Thus we should monitor the relative prices of our current contracts and next period's contract so that we can roll over our position at favorable prices. If we postpone the transaction too long we may be forced to transact at unfavorable prices. Remember that futures contracts trade within a band around their fair value, and the size of the band is determined by arbitrage activity between the contracts and the underlying asset.

PROGRAM TRADING

If for some reason we choose not to employ financial futures when executing asset allocation decisions, we can sometimes execute these decisions in the cash market through program trading. *Program trading* is an arrangement whereby we enter into an agreement with a broker to trade a package of securities. There are many variations of program trading. One important distinction is whether the broker acts as our agent or as a principal. In an *agency trade*, a broker acts as our agent and we assume the risk that the prices may move against us before the transaction is completed. It is common to agree to trade at the market's close, for example. However, if it is known in advance that a large buy order will arrive at the close, traders with this knowledge could move prices up with small orders prior to the close and then sell larger amounts at the inflated closing prices. Of course, this could only happen hypothetically or in the movies, since this activity is illegal.

An alternative to an agency trade is a trade where the broker guarantees prices and thus assumes the risk of transacting at unfavorable prices. In such a trade, the broker acts as a principal and sometimes must sell stocks short if we wish to purchase stocks that are not in the broker's inventory. Over the long run, it is probably cheaper for us to employ a broker as an agent in program trades since brokers charge a premium for acting as a principal. Because they expect to profit from their risk taking, we should end up paying less if we accept the risk. It is extremely unlikely, however, that we can execute as cheaply in the cash market as we can in the futures market.

SUMMARY

- We can usually execute asset allocation decisions more efficiently by trading financial futures than by buying and selling the underlying assets.
- Unless our underlying portfolio is comprised of the indexes or instruments upon which the futures contracts are based, we must adjust the number of contracts we trade to account for our fund's unique systematic risk.
- We can adjust for systematic risk in the equity market by multi-

plying the futures position we would otherwise establish for an index fund by our fund's *beta* (assuming the futures contract is based upon the index).

- For fixed-income investments, we can adjust for systematic risk by multiplying the futures position we would use to hedge a Treasury bond by the ratio of our bond component's duration to the underlying Treasury bond's duration.

- Since futures positions are transacted with borrowed funds, we are required to deposit margin with our broker. Moreover, as the value of our futures position changes each day, we must adjust the amount of our margin.

- As an alternative to trading financial futures, we can arrange with a broker to trade packages of stocks. We can accept the risk of transacting at unfavorable prices by engaging the broker to act as our agent. For a price, however, we can transfer this risk to the broker by requiring guaranteed execution prices.

NOTES

1. Market impact refers to the effect our transaction has on the price. For example, suppose a security traded at $20 on the last trade. If we place a very large order to buy this security and it is not very liquid, we may have to pay substantially more than $20, especially if we demand immediate execution. The increase in price from the last trade induced by our order is referred to as market impact.

2. Actually, these transactions do require a small transfer of capital to cover margin requirements.

3. We can compute the delivery factor for a specific bond by discounting the coupon payments and principal repayment to a present value using a discount rate of 8 percent. The delivery factor equals this present value divided by the bond's face value.

4. For an excellent discussion of the theory and application of financial futures, see S. Figlewski, *Hedging with Financial Futures for Institutional Investors: From Theory to Practice* (Cambridge, Mass. Ballinger Publishing Company, 1986).

5. According to the capital asset pricing model, we should subtract the riskless return from both the market's returns and our portfolio's returns and perform the regression using returns in excess of the riskless return. In most instances, though, we will get similar estimates of *beta* whether or not we adjust for the riskless return.

CHAPTER 10

EVALUATION OF ASSET ALLOCATION STRATEGIES

"There are three kinds of lies: lies, damned lies, and statistics."

Benjamin Disraeli

INTRODUCTION

Suppose we wish to select an investment manager to manage the asset allocation of our fund. We interview several prospective managers, all of whom show us impressive investment results. (Try to imagine an investment manager volunteering unimpressive results.) Some of these results are based on actual experience while some are based on simulations. How can we evaluate these managers?

First, we must establish an appropriate benchmark such as a specific fixed allocation or a rebalancing rule between prespecified asset class indexes. Then, we must distill the performance of the managed portfolio that is due exclusively to the manager's decisions about asset allocation. Finally, we must account for the degree of risk that the manager incurred to achieve the performance. Although these procedures seem simple enough, there are numerous ways in which managers can use statistical methods to mislead us, either intentionally or unwittingly. We will present several examples intended to highlight some of the common pitfalls in the evolution of investment performance due to asset allocation.

SIMULATIONS

Suppose a manager shows us performance based upon a simulation of an asset allocation strategy. Should we be more skeptical of these results than results that are based upon actual experience? Not necessarily. If the simulation was conducted carefully, we might even be justified in attaching more credence to these results than to actual results. Consider, for example, a simulation that is based upon a disciplined investment rule designed to exploit a structurally induced investment opportunity.[1] On the other hand, consider actual results that were generated from a highly subjective decision-making process. We may be perfectly justified in concluding that the results from the disciplined approach are more repeatable than results that depend strongly on someone's ongoing superior judgment. In evaluating the simulation, though, we should take care to ensure that it was conducted correctly.

Hold-Out Period

Suppose a manager shows us asset allocation results based on a simulation covering the last 15 years. The strategy requires that the manager estimate an equilibrium price/earnings multiple for stocks. We recognize that the success of the strategy depends largely on the accuracy of the estimate for the equilibrium price/earnings multiple, so we ask the manager how he estimated this value. He promptly informs us that he used the average value computed over the last 15 years—the same 15 years he used for his simulation. In this case we should regard the simulation with considerable skepticism. The simulation results assume that the manager knew in advance the average value for the price/earnings multiple of stocks. Therefore, the ongoing success of the strategy may depend on information that will not be available to the manager. The manager should have estimated the equilibrium price/earnings multiple from historical data prior to the period he used to test the strategy. Then he should have tested the strategy over a subsequent period called a *hold-out period*.

Significance through Persistence

Suppose that on another interview we meet a manager who presents an asset allocation strategy with impressive results including a *t*-statistic indicating that we should be 95 percent confident that his strategy can add value. This level of confidence normally corresponds to a t-statistic of 2. Suppose we query the manager about the underlying logic of his strategy only to find his explanation somewhat inadequate. As we proceed to question the manager in our best Columbo-like style, he eventually becomes agitated and argues that his strategy is the result of an enormous amount of empirical research. He indicates that he has tested numerous strategies and that this particular strategy is far superior to any of the other approaches he has tested. He goes on to claim that, based on generally accepted statistical procedures, the chances are only 1 in 20 that his strategy will not add value.

If we regard a t-statistic of 2 as persuasive evidence that a strategy will add value, we should ask ourselves or the manager with the strategy a series of simple questions.

First, what are the chances that an arbitrarily chosen strategy will *not* add value with statistical significance? Since the likelihood is only 1 in 20 that an arbitrarily chosen strategy will add value, there is a 95 percent chance that such a strategy will fail to add value.

Next, we should consider the likelihood that neither of two arbitrarily chosen strategies will add value. The answer, of course, is 95 percent squared.[2]

If we proceed along this line of reasoning, we will discover that there is a 49 percent chance that not one of 14 arbitrarily chosen strategies will add value. Thus, if we simulate 14 or more strategies, none of which necessarily have any merit, we should expect that at least one of them will appear to add value with statistical significance merely by random process.

We can illustrate this logic with a simple thought experiment. Suppose there is a group of 1,000 coin tossers. They are asked to toss a fair coin. If it comes up heads, they stay. If it comes up tails they leave. Not surprisingly, after the first toss, 500 hundred of them remain. They toss their coins a second time and 250 of them survive the second cut. After 10 tosses, there is only one coin tosser left who has tossed ten straight heads. The likelihood of tossing 10 consecutive heads is 1 in 1,000. Should we conclude that this person is a skillful coin tosser? What is the likelihood that this expert coin tosser will toss a head on his next toss? The point is that in addition to statistical significance, we should seek evidence that there is some skill embedded in the investment process.

Pooled Data

Suppose we develop a strategy for managing our fund's asset mix. We simulate this strategy over a 10-year period, and we discover that it would have added 4 percent per year with an annual standard deviation of 6 percent. We compute the t-statistic by dividing 6, the standard deviation, by the square root of 10, the number of years in our measurement period, and then by dividing this value into the annual value added of 4 percent.

$$\frac{4}{6/\sqrt{10}} = 2.11$$

We are pleased to find that the t-statistic equals 2.11, which is significant at a confidence level of more than 95 percent. Encouraged by our result, we test our strategy over an earlier, independent 10-year period. In this second simulation covering the earlier period we discover that the strategy added only 2.5 percent per year although its standard deviation was unchanged at 6 percent, yielding a t-statistic of 1.32, which is not statistically significant.

$$\frac{2.5}{6/\sqrt{10}} = 1.32$$

Should we be more or less confident that our strategy can add value after the second simulation? Despite the fact that the second simulation produced a less significant result, we should be more confident that the strategy can add value after the second simulation! Although this answer may seem counterintuitive, we can demonstrate its validity by simulating our strategy over the combined 20-year period. Based on the pooled results, the strategy added 3.25 percent per year with an annual standard deviation of 6 percent. The t-statistic of the strategy equals 2.42, which is significant at a confidence level of 98 percent.

$$\frac{3.25}{6/\sqrt{20}} = 2.42$$

The strategy persisted in adding value for 20 years, which more than offsets the lower value added in the second simulation.[3]

A NONPARAMETRIC EVALUATION
OF ASSET ALLOCATION

Suppose one day you ask your secretary, who is leaving to go out to lunch, to buy a lottery ticket for you. You give him $2 and ask him to choose the number for you. An hour later, your secretary returns with your lottery ticket. The next morning, much to your surprise and joy, you read in the newspaper that you have won $1 million. If you were to apply the industry standard to measure your secretary's investment skills, he would probably rank at the top of any list of professional investment managers. Nonetheless, you would probably not be very inclined to hire your secretary to manage your small fortune.[4] This story illustrates the fact that average value added can be unduly affected by a single event that is not likely to recur. Thus, when we evaluate an asset mix strategy, as a supplement to the magnitude of the value added, we may wish to examine the frequency with which the particular strategy is correct.

In 1981, Robert Merton introduced a *nonparametric* technique for evaluating the skill embedded in asset allocation strategies.[5] To understand Merton's technique, suppose we follow a strategy to allocate a fund between two assets, stocks and bonds. According to Merton, we measure skill by summing the percentage of times the strategy is correct when stocks outperform bonds and the percentage of times the strategy is correct when stocks underperform bonds. A score of 2 indicates perfect timing skill whereas a score of 1 indicates a complete absence of timing skill.

The value of this measurement technique is that it controls for systematic biases in the relative performance of stocks and bonds, or for that matter, any assets. For example, suppose that stocks outperform bonds 70 percent of the time and that this fact is commonly known. An asset allocator who always remained fully invested in stocks would be correct 70 percent of the time, and according to most methods of evaluation, would appear to possess market timing skill. Merton's measure, however, would indicate appropriately that this asset allocator had no skill. He would have been correct 100 percent of the time when stocks outperformed bonds and zero percent of the time when stocks underperformed bonds, for a total score of 1. A score of less than 1 indicates that the strategy or manager is a reverse indicator. In such a situation, the results are probably anomalous, and we are well advised to ignore them.

Of course, a high score using Merton's technique does not necessarily indicate that a strategy will add value. It is conceivable that when the strategy is correct, it is only marginally correct, whereas when it is wrong, it is substantially wrong. Thus we can improve our chances of success in selecting an asset allocation strategy by applying both Merton's technique and measuring the significance of the strategy's value added.

USING MEAN AND VARIANCE TO EVALUATE
DYNAMIC HEDGING STRATEGIES

It is common to compare alternative investment strategies according to their respective expected returns and variances or standard deviations. It is inappropriate, though, to compare a buy-and-hold strategy to a dynamic hedging strategy based strictly on expected return and standard deviation, because these statistics do not adequately describe the return distribution of a dynamic hedging strategy.

Buy-and-hold strategies generate return distributions that are approximately normally distributed, as reflected by the familiar bell-shaped curve. Dynamic hedging strategies, such as portfolio insurance, on the other hand, produce return distributions that are skewed. For example, if we compare portfolio insurance to a 100 percent allocation to a risky asset, the portfolio insurance return distribution is shifted to the left to reflect the cost of the protection (the price of the shadow put option), and the left tail of the distribution is truncated to reflect the protection from returns below the floor value.[6] In Figure 10–1, we show the return distribution for a portfolio insurance strategy superimposed on the return distribution of a 100 percent allocation to a risky asset.

The standard deviation of a dynamic hedging strategy is misleading because most of the variance is concentrated above the mean return; hence high variance is not as undesirable as it would be for a strategy where most of the variance is concentrated below the mean return. Moreover, since other performance statistics such as *alpha* and *beta* are based on standard deviation, they, too, are inadequate to evaluate dynamic hedging strategies.

Although we can quantify the skewness of a return distribution, it may be confusing to compare alternative asset allocation strategies that have different means, variances, and skewness. Perhaps the best approach

FIGURE 10–1
Return Distribution for Portfolio Insurance and Risky Asset

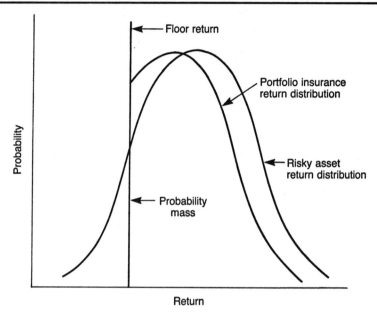

is to trace out the entire return distribution for strategies that are of interest and to evaluate them according to the likelihood they have of achieving our investment objectives.

SUMMARY

- We can easily be misled by a statistical evaluation of asset allocation strategies.
- Although simulated results are not necessarily less reliable than results based upon actual experience, we must take care to ensure that the simulations are conducted correctly. For example, any information used to develop the strategy must have been available

prior to the period used for the simulation. Also, we should be skeptical of results achieved through persistent trials.

- Although results from subperiods may be insignificant, combining these subperiods into a longer measurement period may yield statistically significant results.
- Average value added may be biased by a single, nonrecurring event. As an alternative, we can measure asset allocation skill by summing the percentage of times a strategy is correct when an asset outperforms and the percentage of times the strategy is correct when an asset underperforms. This approach controls for commonly known biases in an asset's relative performance.
- Evaluation techniques based on mean and variance are inadequate for evaluating dynamic hedging strategies, since their return distributions are not symmetric.

NOTES

1. We intentionally avoided the word "inefficiency," since proponents of market efficiency have revised the definition of efficiency in the face of overwhelming evidence to the contrary. Thus we now have anomalies and multiple asset pricing models and joint hypotheses, but still no inefficiencies.
2. In this example, we assume implicitly that arbitrarily chosen strategies are mutually independent.
3. Of course, if we believe that for some reason the circumstances associated with the period that produced the lower t-statistic are more likely to be repeated than the circumstances from the period with the higher t-statistic, we may be correct in feeling less confident about our strategy.
4. This example was told to me by Robert Merton.
5. R. Merton, "On Market Timing and Investment Performance: 1. An Equilibrium Theory of Value for Market Forecasts," *Journal of Business* 54, no. 3 (1981), pp. 363–405.
6. For an excellent discussion of this issue, see R. Bookstaber and R. Clarke, "Problems in Evaluating the Performance of Portfolios with Options," *Financial Analysts Journal* (January/February 1985), pp. 48–62.

AMERICAN FABRIC: PART 3

Several months have passed since Betsy Ross' successful asset allocation presentation to the Investment Committee. The fund's asset mix has been revised in accordance with her recommendation, and investment performance is quite good. Betsy was exploring the merits of international diversification when she was interrupted by Tom Paine. Let us rejoin Betsy Ross at American Fabric.

Betsy had just received a call from Tom Paine's secretary requesting that she meet with Mr. Paine the next morning at 10:30 in his office. Betsy had no idea what this meeting was about. As far as she could recall, the investment performance of the pension fund was quite satisfactory and there were no urgent issues that needed to be addressed. She had just begun to explore the merits of diversifying part of the assets into foreign investments, but it was much too early for Mr. Paine to expect any substantive report on that project. "Well, I guess I shouldn't worry," thought Betsy, "but I just wish I knew what was on his mind."

Betsy reported to Paine's office promptly at 10:30 the following morning and was told to go right in.

"Good morning, Betsy. I'm glad that you could meet with me on such short notice. I hope I didn't interfere with anything important."

"Not at all, Mr. Paine," responded Betsy. "I was working on a project to evaluate the merits of international diversification."

"Well, Betsy, I encourage you to pursue that project, but right now I'm afraid that I need you to look into another matter for me. There are two members of our board that sit on boards of other companies that have used portfolio insurance. Now I realize that portfolio insurance was criticized quite severely after the crash, but I'm not convinced that it performed as poorly as some of the critics would have us believe. Maybe it didn't work perfectly, but from what I've heard, most insured portfolios performed a lot better than uninsured portfolios. In any event, I'm getting pressure to insure our pension assets. Betsy, I would like you to review portfolio insurance to determine whether or not we should insure our assets. I would like you to prepare a report and a recommendation for our Investment Committee next month. I'm intrigued by this strategy, but I'm not sure whether I should believe those who promote it as a free lunch or its critics who blame it for everything, including the stock market crash. I suspect the truth lies somewhere in between."

"I'll be happy to look into portfolio insurance for you, Mr. Paine," said Betsy. "I believe there is a great deal of confusion about this topic, based on discussions I've had with my contacts in the industry. And my suspicion is that much of this confusion is the result of both overly enthusiastic vendors of the product and portfolio managers trying to rationalize their poor results."

"Betsy, do I detect a tone of cynicism?" asked Paine.

"Mr. Paine, I hope I haven't become cynical. I really try to maintain an open mind. But sometimes I wonder how people get away with the claims they make."

"I understand your concern, Betsy. I also believe that a cautious attitude is appropriate. But don't let a few overly enthusiastic salespeople, as you so generously describe them, distort your view of the industry."

Although Betsy was engrossed in her investigation of foreign investment, she welcomed the opportunity to evaluate portfolio insurance. She remembered how much notoriety the strategy had attracted after the crash, but she never had a chance to review it thoroughly. Given its historic significance, she felt compelled to understand the strategy. She began by reviewing the binomial option pricing model introduced by William Sharpe, since she realized that portfolio insurance was based upon the arbitrage arguments that underlie option valuation. Once she felt comfortable with the correspondence between option valuation and portfolio insurance, she wrote a simple computer program using the Black-Scholes continuous-time model to simulate portfolio insurance. She was interested primarily in determining the sensitivity of the results to the frequency of trading. In just a few days, Betsy felt that she had a sound understanding of the theoretical, as well as procedural, issues surrounding portfolio insurance. In fact, she was quite perplexed about why there seemed to be so much confusion about the strategy. Portfolio insurance seemed fairly straightforward to her.

Before preparing her report, Betsy thought it would be a good idea to review some of the promotional literature for portfolio insurance. She called the main vendors and asked them to send her whatever material they were willing to share with her. Although they all tried to arrange a meeting with her, she convinced them that her interest was very preliminary, promising to meet with them if she decided to proceed with portfolio insurance. As soon as she reviewed the promotional material, she understood immediately why the industry was so confused. A popular ploy among some of the vendors, although not all of them, was to compare portfolio insurance to an alternative buy-and-hold strategy that was selected conveniently to enhance the comparative attractiveness of portfolio insurance. One brochure, for example, claimed that for the same downside risk of a buy-and-hold strategy an investor could increase a portfolio's expected return by implementing a portfolio insurance strategy. Although Betsy realized that in some cases this claim may be true technically, she immediately realized that the comparison was not valid. Portfolio insurance is a dynamic hedging strategy which generates a skewed distribution of potential outcomes. Buy-and-hold strategies generate approximately symmetric return distributions. By comparing only the expected return and another conveniently selected point along the return distribution, it is possible to contrive a comparison where either strategy appears superior. Betsy thought it would be amusing to propose a strategy whereby the portfolio insurance vendor would sell short the buy-and-hold strategy and invest in the portfolio insurance strategy. Would this vendor agree to guarantee the profits of such an arbitrage? Of course, she knew the answer.

Betsy realized that most of the Committee members were unfamiliar with many of the nuances that enabled her to uncover the subterfuge in some of the promotional literature. She decided that the best approach for her presentation would be pictures. First, she prepared a payoff diagram of three buy-and-hold strategies: a 100 percent investment in a risky asset, a 100 percent investment in a riskless asset, and a 50/50 mix between a risky asset and a riskless asset. Next, she prepared a payoff diagram of a portfolio insurance strategy. Finally, she prepared an exhibit overlaying a portfolio insurance payoff function on a buy-and-hold payoff function. Betsy was confident that with these exhibits she would be able to offer a fair and comprehensible comparison of portfolio insurance and alternative buy-and-hold strategies.

At the Investment Committee meeting, Betsy began her presentation by reviewing the history of portfolio insurance and then explaining its correspondence with option strategies. She then read some of the claims from the promotional literature focusing on the comparison between portfolio insurance and buy-and-hold strategies. She expressed her opinion that once the Committee understood the tradeoffs between these two investment strategies they would be in a position to choose which approach coincided with their attitude toward risk.

Betsy began with the payoff diagram for the buy-and-hold strategies. She explained that the horizontal axis represented various potential values for the risky asset while the vertical axis represented the corresponding returns of the three alternative strategies. She emphasized that any buy-and-hold strategy between a risky asset and a riskless asset could be represented by a straight line payoff function. She also pointed out that the

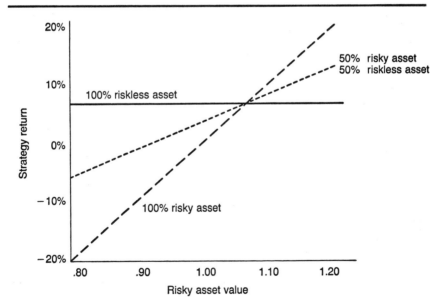

Betsy's Payoff Diagram of Buy-and-Hold Strategies

steeper the slope of the line, the higher the percentage allocated to the risky asset.

Next, Betsy showed them the payoff diagram of a portfolio insurance strategy superimposed on a payoff diagram representing 100 percent investment in a risky asset. She pointed out all of the popular analogies between portfolio insurance and conventional insurance.

After she was confident that the Committee understood this exhibit, Betsy explained that some buy-and-hold strategies also provide a high level of certainty of exceeding a minimum required return. In fact, she argued, when you consider the estimation risk and potential slippage from execution associated with portfolio insurance, some buy-and-hold strategies offered as much downside protection as portfolio insurance.

At this point one of the Committee members interrupted Betsy. "But according to this brochure, portfolio insurance has a higher expected return than a buy-and-hold strategy with equivalent downside protection. It seems obvious that portfolio insurance is a superior strategy."

Betsy's Payoff Diagram of Portfolio Insurance

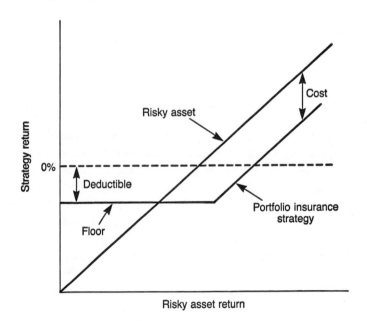

Betsy couldn't have hoped for a better introduction to her next exhibit, especially since this particular committee member had regularly interrupted her with irrelevant criticisms.

"I'm glad you raised this issue," said Betsy confidently, yet with deference. Already she could see his expression change from arrogance to concern, since he knew that Betsy was always prepared.

Betsy referred the Committee to her final exhibit where she had superimposed a portfolio insurance strategy payoff function on a buy-and-hold payoff function representing an equal allocation to a risky and a riskless asset. Betsy explained that, based on the expected returns and standard deviations of the risky and riskless assets and their correlation, the buy-and-hold strategy had a 99 percent chance of producing a return equal to or greater than −5 percent. She then pointed out that the portfolio insurance strategy had a floor of −5 percent. She continued to explain that she had simulated this strategy and that, in fact, based upon realistic assumptions regarding the frequency of rebalancing and estimation error, the portfolio insurance strategy had about a 1 percent chance of penetrating the floor. Thus she concluded that the two strategies had equivalent downside protection. The Committee agreed with Betsy's reasoning so far.

"Now," said Betsy, "I would like to demonstrate why it is not always valid to evaluate strategies based upon only two potential outcomes. As you can see from this exhibit, the portfolio insurance strategy has a higher expected return than the buy-and-hold strategy's expected return. However, there is a wide range of outcomes for the risky asset where the buy-and-hold strategy has a higher corresponding return than the portfolio insurance strategy."

Betsy continued, "If one wished to promote a buy-and-hold strategy, it would be quite simple to contrive a comparison of two potential outcomes where the buy-and-hold strategy seemed superior. The point is that when we compare a buy-and-hold strategy to a dynamic strategy, we must examine the entire distribution of potential returns of both strategies in order to render a valid comparison. I am not arguing that you should reject portfolio insurance. That depends on your attitude toward risk. I do recommend, though, that you consider the consequences of such a strategy on the net worth of the pension fund."

Betsy then launched into a comparison of insuring the assets versus insuring the fund's net worth, and she introduced an alternative dynamic

Betsy's Comparison of Portfolio Insurance and a Buy-and-Hold Strategy

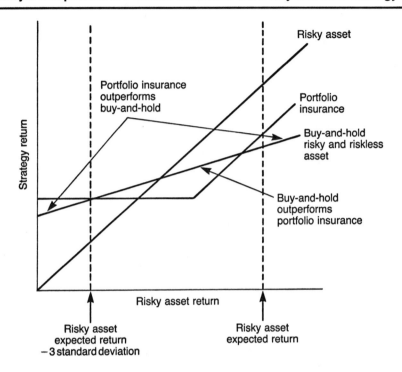

hedging strategy called constant proportion portfolio insurance. By the end of the meeting, although the Committee couldn't reach a decision about portfolio insurance, they were convinced of Betsy's expertise on the topic and of her value to American Fabric.

APPENDIXES

APPENDIX A

OPTIMIZATION PROCEDURES

In order to identify the actual asset weights that form the portfolios along the efficient frontier, we need to minimize risk for each level of expected return. For convenience (primarily the author's), we will first assume that our portfolio includes only two assets. In order to find the efficient portfolios, we must begin by specifying an objective function.

$$z = S^2_1 \cdot W^2_1 + S^2_2 \cdot W^2_2 + 2 \cdot r_{1,2} \cdot S_1 \cdot W_1 \cdot S_2 \cdot W_2 +$$
$$\lambda_1 \cdot (R_1 \cdot W_1 + R_2 \cdot W_2 - R_P) +$$
$$\lambda_2 \cdot (W_1 + W_2 - 1)$$

where

z = Objective function
S_1 = Standard deviation of asset 1
S_2 = Standard deviation of asset 2
W_1 = Percent invested in asset 1
W_2 = Percent invested in asset 2
$r_{1,2}$ = Correlation coefficient between asset 1 and asset 2
R_1 = Expected return of asset 1
R_2 = Expected return of asset 2
R_P = Expected return of portfolio
λ_1 = Lagrange multiplier for first constraint
λ_2 = Lagrange multiplier for second constraint

The first line of this objective function is precisely equivalent to portfolio variance. The second line is a constraint to ensure that the weighted average of the component assets' returns equals the portfolio's total return. The third line is a second constraint to ensure that the asset weights sum to 1.

We can minimize this objective function by taking the following partial derivatives, setting them equal to zero, and solving for the asset weights.

$$\delta z/\delta W_1 = 2 \cdot S^2_1 \cdot W_1 + 2 \cdot r_{1,2} \cdot S_1 \cdot S_2 \cdot W_2 + \lambda_1 \cdot R_1 + \lambda_2 = 0$$
$$\delta z/\delta W_2 = 2 \cdot S^2_2 \cdot W_2 + 2 \cdot r_{1,2} \cdot S_1 \cdot W_1 \cdot S_2 + \lambda_1 \cdot R_2 + \lambda_2 = 0$$
$$\delta z/\delta \lambda_1 = R_1 \cdot W_1 + R_2 \cdot W_2 - R_p = 0$$
$$\delta z/\delta \lambda_2 = W_1 + W_2 - 1 = 0$$

Using matrix notation, we can represent the above linear equations by the coefficient matrix, weight vector, and constraint vector shown below.

$$
\begin{bmatrix}
2 \cdot S_1^2 & 2 \cdot r_{1,2} \cdot S_1 \cdot S_2 & R_1 & 1 \\
2 \cdot r_{1,2} \cdot S_1 \cdot S_2 & 2 \cdot S_2^2 & R_2 & 1 \\
R_1 & R_2 & 0 & 0 \\
1 & 1 & 0 & 0
\end{bmatrix}
\begin{bmatrix}
W_1 \\
W_2 \\
\lambda_1 \\
\lambda_2
\end{bmatrix}
=
\begin{bmatrix}
0 \\
0 \\
R_p \\
1
\end{bmatrix}
$$

We can solve this system of linear equations by using Cramer's Rule.[1] We simply need to find the determinant of the coefficient matrix, the determinant of the coefficient matrix substituting the constraint vector for column 1, and the determinant of the coefficient matrix substituting the constraint vector for column 2.

It may be useful to demonstrate this procedure with a numerical example. Suppose asset 1 has an expected return of 12 percent and a standard deviation of 20 percent, while asset 2 has an expected return of 8 percent and a standard deviation of 10 percent. Further, suppose that the returns of asset 1 and asset 2 are 15 percent correlated with each other.

With these assumptions, the determinant of the coefficient matrix equals:

$$
\begin{vmatrix}
.08 & .006 & .12 & 1.00 \\
.006 & .02 & .08 & 1.00 \\
.12 & .08 & 0.00 & 0.00 \\
1.00 & 1.00 & 0.00 & 0.00
\end{vmatrix} = .0016
$$

Similarly, the determinant of the coefficient matrix with the constraint vector substituted for column 1 equals:

$$
\begin{vmatrix}
0.00 & .006 & .12 & 1.00 \\
0.00 & .02 & .08 & 1.00 \\
R & .08 & 0.00 & 0.00 \\
1.00 & 1.00 & 0.00 & 0.00
\end{vmatrix} = -.0032 + .04 \cdot R_p
$$

Finally, the determinant of the coefficient matrix with the constraint vector substituted for column 2 equals:

$$\begin{vmatrix} .08 & 0.00 & .12 & 1.00 \\ .006 & 0.00 & .08 & 1.00 \\ .12 & R & 0.00 & 0.00 \\ 1.00 & 1.00 & 0.00 & 0.00 \end{vmatrix} = -.04 \cdot R_P + .0048$$

According to Cramer's Rule, for any given portfolio expected return, the percent to invest in asset 1 to yield the minimum risk portfolio equals the second determinant divided by the first determinant:

$$W_1 = \frac{-.0032 -.04 \cdot R_p}{.0016} = -2 + 25 \cdot R_p$$

while the percent to invest in asset 2 equals the third determinant divided by the first determinant:

$$W_2 = \frac{-.04 \cdot R_p + .0048}{.0016} = 3 - 25 \cdot R_p$$

By substituting various levels of portfolio expected return into these equations, we can determine the asset weights that yield the minimum risk portfolio for each level of expected return.

This approach is limited in an important way. If our portfolio includes more than two assets, it is quite likely that some of the efficient portfolios will include negative positions in one or more of the assets, indicating that we must sell these assets short. However, many institutional investors are proscribed from short selling. Unfortunately, within the framework we have just described, we cannot accommodate constraints that are specified as "greater than or equal to," which is the type of constraint needed to control short selling, since calculus solutions require equalities.

As an alternative to this approach, we can find the efficient portfolios by employing an iterative procedure introduced by William Sharpe.[2] Suppose we redefine our objective as follows:

$$z = R_1 \cdot W_1 + R_2 \cdot W_2 + R_3 + W_3 - \lambda(S^2_1 \cdot W^2_1 + S^2_2 + W^2_2 + S^2_3 \cdot W^2_3$$
$$+ 2 \cdot r_{1,2} \cdot S_1 \cdot W_1 \cdot S_2 \cdot W_2 + 2 \cdot r_{1,3} \cdot S_1 \cdot W_1 \cdot S_3 \cdot W_3$$
$$+ 2 \cdot r_{2,3} \cdot S_2 \cdot W_2 \cdot S_3 \cdot W_3)$$

where

z = Objective function

R_1 = Expected return of asset 1

R_2 = Expected return of asset 2

R_3 = Expected return of asset 3

S_1 = Standard deviation of asset 1

S_2 = Standard deviation of asset 2

S_3 = Standard deviation of asset 3

W_1 = Percent invested in asset 1

W_2 = Percent invested in asset 2

W_3 = Percent invested in asset 3

$r_{1,2}$ = Correlation coefficient between asset 1 and asset 2

$r_{1,3}$ = Correlation coefficient between asset 1 and asset 3

$r_{2,3}$ = Correlation coefficient between asset 2 and asset 3

λ = Risk aversion parameter (our willingness to sacrifice one unit of expected return in order to reduce risk by one unit)

Again, we take the derivative of our objective function with respect to each asset weight, which we show below for asset 1.

$$\delta z / \delta W_1 = R_1 - \lambda (2 \cdot S^2_1 W_1 + 2 \cdot r_{1,2} \cdot S_1 \cdot W_2 \cdot S_2 + 2 \cdot r_{1,3} \cdot S_1 \cdot W_3 \cdot S_3)$$

Now, in order to find the efficient portfolios, given our aversion to risk, we simply follow an iterative procedure whereby we increase the allocation to the asset that has the highest derivative and reduce, by the same amount, the asset with the lowest derivative, subject to any constraints we may wish to impose for the asset weights. When all of the derivatives are equal to each other (again, subject to our constraints), we cannot improve the portfolio any further; hence we have found the asset weights that maximize our objective function.

NOTES

1. We can also find the asset's weights by inverting the coefficient matrix and multiplying it by the constraint vector. Cramer's Rule is a short cut that will yield the same answer. For a review of Cramer's Rule, see A. Chaing, *Fundamental Methods of Mathematical Economics* (New York: McGraw-Hill, 1974).

2. W. F. Sharpe, "An Algorithm for Portfolio Improvement" (Research Paper No. 475, Graduate School of Business, Stanford University, October, 1978).

APPENDIX B

NORMAL DISTRIBUTION TABLE
AND HOW TO USE IT

Suppose our target return equals 9 percent, our expected return equals 12 percent, and the standard deviation of returns equals 20 percent. We calculate z as:

$$z = \frac{.09 - .12}{.20} = -.15$$

In order to find the probability that the expected return will equal or exceed the target return, we look up the value, $-.15$, in the Normal Distribution Table on pp. 180-181. We go down the left column to -0.1 and across to the column under $-.05$. This value, .4404, equals the probability that the target return will equal or exceed the expected return. One minus this value, or .5596, equals the probability that the expected return will equal or exceed the target return.

If, instead, our target return equals 12 percent, our expected return equals 9 percent, and the standard deviation of returns equals 20 percent, we calculate z as:

$$z = \frac{.12 - .09}{.20} = .15$$

If we look up the value, .15, in the Normal Distribution Table, we find that there is a .5596 probability that the target return will equal or exceed the expected return. Thus, one minus this value, or .4404, equals the probability that the expected return will equal or exceed the target return.

NORMAL DISTRIBUTION TABLE
Probability Target Outcome > = Expected Outcome

z	−.00	−.01	−.02	−.03	−.04	−.05	−.06	−.07	−.08	−.09
−3.0	.0013	.0013	.0013	.0012	.0012	.0011	.0011	.0011	.0010	.0010
−2.9	.0019	.0018	.0018	.0017	.0017	.0016	.0015	.0015	.0014	.0014
−2.8	.0026	.0025	.0024	.0023	.0023	.0022	.0021	.0021	.0020	.0019
−2.7	.0035	.0034	.0033	.0032	.0031	.0030	.0029	.0028	.0027	.0026
−2.6	.0047	.0045	.0044	.0043	.0041	.0040	.0039	.0038	.0037	.0036
−2.5	.0062	.0060	.0059	.0057	.0055	.0054	.0052	.0051	.0049	.0048
−2.4	.0082	.0080	.0078	.0075	.0073	.0071	.0069	.0068	.0066	.0064
−2.3	.0107	.0104	.0102	.0099	.0096	.0094	.0091	.0089	.0087	.0084
−2.2	.0139	.0136	.0132	.0129	.0125	.0122	.0119	.0116	.0113	.0110
−2.1	.0179	.0174	.0170	.0166	.0162	.0158	.0154	.0150	.0146	.0143
−2.0	.0228	.0222	.0217	.0212	.0207	.0202	.0197	.0192	.0188	.0183
−1.9	.0287	.0281	.0275	.0268	.0262	.0256	.0250	.0244	.0239	.0233
−1.8	.0359	.0351	.0344	.0336	.0329	.0322	.0314	.0307	.0300	.0294
−1.7	.0446	.0436	.0427	.0418	.0409	.0401	.0392	.0384	.0375	.0367
−1.6	.0548	.0537	.0526	.0516	.0505	.0495	.0485	.0475	.0465	.0455
−1.5	.0668	.0655	.0643	.0630	.0618	.0606	.0594	.0582	.0571	.0560
−1.4	.0808	.0793	.0778	.0764	.0750	.0735	.0721	.0708	.0694	.0681
−1.3	.0968	.0951	.0934	.0918	.0901	.0885	.0869	.0853	.0838	.0823
−1.2	.1151	.1131	.1112	.1093	.1075	.1056	.1038	.1020	.1003	.0985
−1.1	.1357	.1335	.1314	.1292	.1271	.1251	.1230	.1210	.1190	.1170
−1.0	.1587	.1562	.1539	.1515	.1492	.1469	.1446	.1423	.1401	.1379
−0.9	.1841	.1814	.1788	.1762	.1736	.1711	.1685	.1660	.1635	.1611
−0.8	.2119	.2090	.2061	.2033	.2005	.1977	.1949	.1921	.1894	.1867
−0.7	.2420	.2389	.2358	.2327	.2296	.2266	.2236	.2206	.2177	.2148
−0.6	.2743	.2709	.2676	.2643	.2611	.2578	.2546	.2514	.2483	.2451
−0.5	.3085	.3050	.3015	.2981	.2946	.2912	.2877	.2843	.2810	.2776
−0.4	.3446	.3400	.3372	.3336	.3300	.3264	.3228	.3192	.3156	.3121
−0.3	.3821	.3783	.3745	.3707	.3669	.3632	.3594	.3557	.3520	.3483
−0.2	.4207	.4168	.4129	.4090	.4052	.4013	.3974	.3936	.3897	.3859
−0.1	.4602	.4562	.4522	.4483	.4443	.4404	.4364	.4325	.4286	.4247
−0.0	.5000	.4960	.4920	.4880	.4840	.4801	.4761	.4721	.4681	.4641
0.0	.5000	.5040	.5080	.5120	.5160	.5199	.5239	.5279	.5319	.5359
0.1	.5398	.5438	.5478	.5517	.5557	.5596	.5636	.5675	.5714	.5753
0.2	.5793	.5832	.5871	.5910	.5948	.5897	.6026	.6064	.6103	.6141
0.3	.6179	.6217	.6255	.6293	.6331	.6368	.6406	.6443	.6480	.6517
0.4	.6554	.6592	.6628	.6664	.6700	.6736	.6772	.6808	.6844	.6880
0.5	.6915	.6950	.6985	.7019	.7054	.7088	.7123	.7157	.7190	.7224
0.6	.7257	.7291	.7324	.7357	.7389	.7422	.7454	.7486	.7517	.7549
0.7	.7580	.7611	.7642	.7673	.7704	.7734	.7764	.7794	.7823	.7852
0.8	.7881	.7910	.7939	.7967	.7995	.8023	.8051	.8078	.8106	.8133
0.9	.8159	.8186	.8212	.8238	.8264	.8289	.8315	.8340	.8365	.8389
1.0	.8413	.8438	.8461	.8485	.8508	.8531	.8554	.8577	.8599	.8621
1.1	.8643	.8665	.8686	.8708	.8729	.8749	.8770	.8790	.8810	.8830

Continued

NORMAL DISTRIBUTION TABLE *Concluded*

1.2	.8849	.8870	.8888	.8907	.8925	.8944	.8962	.8980	.8997	.9015
1.3	.9032	.9049	.9066	.9082	.9099	.9115	.9131	.9147	.9162	.9177
1.4	.9192	.9207	.9222	.9236	.9251	.9265	.9279	.9292	.9306	.9319
1.5	.9332	.9345	.9357	.9370	.9382	.9394	.9406	.9418	.9429	.9441
1.6	.9452	.9463	.9474	.9484	.9495	.9505	.9515	.9525	.9535	.9545
1.7	.9554	.0564	.9573	.9582	.9591	.9599	.9608	.9616	.9625	.9633
1.8	.9641	.9649	.9656	.9664	.9671	.9678	.9686	.9693	.9700	.9706
1.9	.9713	.9719	.9726	.9732	.9738	.9744	.9750	.9756	.9761	.9767
2.0	.9772	.9778	.9783	.9788	.9793	.9798	.9803	.9808	.9812	.9817
2.1	.9821	.9826	.9830	.9834	.9838	.9842	.9846	.9850	.9854	.9857
2.2	.9861	.9864	.9868	.9871	.9875	.9878	.9881	.9884	.9887	.9890
2.3	.9893	.9896	.9898	.9901	.9904	.9906	.9909	.9911	.9913	.9916
2.4	.9918	.9920	.9922	.9925	.9927	.9929	.9931	.9932	.9934	.9936
2.5	.9938	.9940	.9941	.9943	.9945	.9946	.9948	.9949	.9951	.9952
2.6	.9953	.9955	.9956	.9957	.9959	.9960	.9961	.9962	.9963	.9964
2.7	.9965	.9966	.9967	.9968	.9969	.9970	.9971	.9972	.9973	.9974
2.8	.9974	.9975	.9976	.9977	.9977	.9978	.9979	.9979	.9980	.9981
2.9	.9981	.9982	.9982	.9983	.9984	.9984	.9985	.9985	.9986	.9987
3.0	.9987	.9987	.9987	.9988	.9988	.9989	.9989	.9989	.9990	.9990

APPENDIX C

NUMERICAL APPROXIMATION FOR NORMAL DISTRIBUTION

As an alternative to a Normal Distribution Table, there are several algorithms that we can use to find the area under a curve that corresponds to a particular z value. These algorithms are useful in that they can easily be incorporated into spreadsheet software. We present one such algorithm below.

Let z' equal:

$$\text{absolute value of } z$$

Let r equal:

$$1 + z' \cdot (C_1 + z' \cdot (C_2 + z' \cdot (C_3 + z' \cdot (C_4 + z' \cdot (C_5 + z' \cdot C_6)))))$$

where,

$C_1 = .049867347$	$C_4 = .0000380036$
$C_2 = .0211410061$	$C_5 = .0000488906$
$C_3 = .0032776263$	$C_6 = .000005383$

Let P (probability that target return will equal or exceed expected return) equal:

$$.5 \cdot e^{(\ln (r) \cdot (-16))}$$

If $z \geq 0$, $P = 1 - P$

To demonstrate this algorithm, suppose that $z = -.15$. If we substitute this value into our equation for r, we find that r equals 1.0079668597 (approximately).

$$1 + .15 \cdot (.049867347 + .15 \cdot (.0211410061 + .15 \cdot (.0032776263 + .15 \cdot$$
$$(.0000380036 + .15 \cdot (.0000488906 + .15 \cdot (.000005383)))) = 1.0079668597$$

If we substitute r into our equation for P, we find that P equals. 44038, since z is less than 0.

$$.5 \cdot e^{(ln\,(1.0079668597)\,\cdot\,(-16))} = .44038$$

Note that the value corresponding to $-.15$ in the Normal Distribution Table in Appendix B equals .4404.

APPENDIX D

NEWTON RAPHSON METHOD

When iteration is necessary to find the solution to a problem, we can save time by employing a search procedure that minimizes the number of iterations required to arrive at the answer. One such procedure is called the Newton Raphson Method. We will demonstrate this procedure by applying it to find the implied volatility from the price of an option.

Recall from Chapter 2 that the value of an option is determined by the price of the underlying asset, the strike price, the volatility (standard deviation) of the underlying asset, the riskless rate of interest, and the time remaining to expiration. All of these values are known, with the exception of the volatility of the underlying asset. Therefore, by observing the price at which an option trades, we can substitute different values for volatility until the value of the option consistent with our estimate of volatility equals the option's reported price.

According to the Newton Raphson Method, we start with some reasonable estimate for volatility and evaluate the option according to this estimate. Unless our estimate yields the option's price, we change our estimate by an amount equal to the option value, given our estimate for volatility minus the option's current price, divided by the derivative of the option price with respect to volatility evaluated at our estimate for volatility.

The value of an option can be written as:

$$1 \quad C = R \cdot N(D) - Kr^{-T} \cdot N(D - S \cdot \sqrt{T})$$

$$2 \quad D = ln(R/Kr^{-T}) + 1/2 \cdot S \cdot \sqrt{T}$$

where
- C = Value of call option
- R = Value of risky asset
- K = Strike price
- r = One plus the riskless rate of interest

S = Standard deviation of risky asset

T = Time remaining to expiration

N( ) = Cumulative normal density function

The derivative of the value of a call option with respect to the volatility of the underlying asset equals:

$$\delta C / \delta S = R \cdot \sqrt{T} \cdot (1/\sqrt{2\pi}) e^{-D^2/2}$$

To illustrate how the Newton Raphson Method works, suppose that we observe in the newspaper that a call option with a strike price of $295 due to expire in 90 days on an underlying asset valued at $300 traded for $15.00. Also, suppose that the riskless rate of interest for the subsequent 90 days equals 8 percent, and that the historical volatility of the underlying asset for the preceding 90 days was 20 percent.

We start by finding the value for this option assuming that the volatility of the underlying asset equals 20 percent. If we substitute the above values, along with our volatility estimate of 20 percent, into the option pricing formula, we find that the option's fair value is $17.69, which is greater than the price at which the option traded. Hence, we change our volatility estimate according to the following formula:

$$S_{i+1} = S_i - (\hat{C} - C)/C'$$

where

S_{i+1} = New estimate for volatility

s_1 = Current estimate for volatility

C = Reported price of option

$\hat{C}$ = Value of option based on current estimate for volatility

C' = Derivative of option price with respect to volatility evaluated at current estimate for volatility

By substitution, we find that our new estimate for volatility equals 15.07 percent, which yields an option value of $15.06. With one more iteration, our estimate for volatility equals 14.96 percent, which yields an option price of $15.00, the exact price we observed in the newspaper.

GLOSSARY

A

agency trade A trade in which the broker does not assume any principal risk, but instead acts as an agent for the buyer or seller.

arbitrage A process whereby profits are earned by exchanging assets without incurring risk. For example, an arbitrageur can buy futures contracts when they sell at a discount to their fair value and simultaneously sell short the underlying asset. At expiration their prices would be equal so that the arbitrageur could realize the initial spread by receiving the cash for the futures contracts and, with these proceeds, cover the short position.

B

beta A measure of an asset's sensitivity to an underlying index or factor. For example, an asset with a *beta* equal to 1.2 would be expected to return 12 percent if the index returned 10 percent and −12 percent if the index returned −10 percent.

binomial option pricing model A valuation model for options which assumes that changes in asset prices follow a binomial distribution in that prices can increase or decrease only by certain specified amounts, with certain probability. The value of the option is computed by beginning with the values at the end of the binomial tree and working backwards to solve for the option's value at the beginning of the binomial tree. This model assumes that prices change discretely rather than continuously and that an asset's value can only move up or down in the next period.

Black-Scholes option pricing model A valuation model for options which assumes that asset prices change continuously and that investors cannot earn riskless profits. According to the Black-Scholes model, the value of an option depends on the price of the underlying asset, the strike price, the riskless return, the standard deviation of the underlying asset, and the time remaining to expiration.

buy-and-hold strategy A strategy whereby an asset mix is bought and left unchanged throughout the investment horizon. It is not rebalanced to the initial mix. Buy-and-hold strategies are represented by straight line payoff functions.

C

call option A contract that gives the owner the right but not the obligation to purchase an asset at a prespecified strike price for a prespecified period of time.

concave payoff function In a payoff diagram, a payoff that increases at a decreasing rate with the value of the underlying risky asset. Strategies that buy low and sell high, such as rebalancing strategies, produce concave payoff functions.

constant proportion portfolio insurance (CPPI) A dynamic hedging strategy designed to prevent a portfolio from penetrating a prespecified value. This strategy is a time-invariant alternative to portfolio insurance. It is implemented by multiplying the difference between the portfolio value and the floor value by a multiple greater than 1 and allocating this amount to a risky asset with the balance allocated to a riskless asset.

convex payoff function In a payoff diagram, a payoff that increases at an increasing rate with the value of the underlying risky asset. Strategies that buy high and sell low, such as portfolio insurance, produce convex payoff functions.

correlation coefficient A measure (ranging in value from −1 to 1) of the association between a dependent variable and one or more independent variables. A correlation coefficient is not necessarily a measure of causality but rather the strength of a relationship. A correlation coefficient of 1 implies that the variables move perfectly in lockstep; a correlation of −1 implies that the variables move inversely in lockstep; a correlation of 0 implies that the variables, as calibrated, are uncorrelated.

cost of carry In valuing a financial futures contract, the interest cost associated with purchasing the underlying asset on margin.

covariance A measure of the extent to which a pair of variables moves together. It is computed as the average distance from the mean of one variable times the average distance from the mean of the other variable.

cushion In a constant proportion portfolio insurance strategy, the difference between the portfolio value and the floor value.

D

deductible In a portfolio insurance strategy, the difference between the portfolio value and the floor value.

delivery factor In valuing a Treasury bond futures contract, a factor which equates a deliverable bond to a 20-year bond with a coupon yield of 8 percent. The delivery factor equals the present value of the deliverable bond, based on a discount rate of 8 percent, divided by the bond's face value.

delta In option valuation, the fraction of the risky asset that hedges an investment in a call option on the risky asset. It also measures the sensitivity of the option value to changes in the value of the underlying asset.

duration The average time to receipt of cash flows weighted by their present values. It measures the sensitivity of a bond's price to a change in interest rates, and it is computed as the first derivative of bond price with respect to interest rates.

dynamic hedging strategy A strategy in which a portfolio's asset mix is shifted between a risky asset and a riskless asset in response to changes in the value of the portfolio, so as to protect the portfolio from declining below a prespecified value. Funds are allocated to a risky asset as the portfolio's value rises and to a riskless asset as the portfolio's value falls. Portfolio insurance and constant proportion portfolio insurance are examples of dynamic hedging strategies.

E

e The mathematical constant equal to 2.718282 that is the value of $1 compounded continuously for one year at a rate of 100 percent. *e* is used to compute a continuously compounded return by raising its value to the power of the simple return and subtracting 1.

efficient frontier In dimensions of expected return and standard deviation, a continuum of efficient portfolios (see *efficient portfolio*, below).

efficient portfolio A portfolio that has the highest expected return for a given level of risk or, alternatively, a portfolio that has the lowest risk for a given level of expected return.

embedded currency exposure The exposure to a currency that arises from translating the return of a foreign investment to a domestic return.

expected return An estimate of return for which there is a 50 percent probability of experiencing an actual return that is above or below this estimate.

E-V maxim (*expected return-variance maxim*)   A rule for selecting investments which states that investors should choose portfolios with the highest level of expected return at each level of variance.

F

floor   In a portfolio insurance strategy, a prespecified minimum value that the insured portfolio is protected from penetrating (in theory).

foreign exchange risk   When investing in foreign markets, the risk that the currency of that country will depreciate against the domestic country's currency and thereby lower the return on the foreign investment.

forward contract   A contract, privately negotiated between two parties, that obligates the seller to pay the value of the contract to the buyer at a prespecified date.

futures contract   A contract, with uniform terms concerning price, quantity, and expiration, which obligates the seller to pay the value of the contract to the buyer at a prespecified date.

H

hedge ratio   In a portfolio insurance strategy, the percentage of the insured portfolio that is allocated to the risky asset.

heuristic   A problem-solving approach in which one proceeds along empirical lines, using rules of thumb to arrive at a solution.

hold-out period   In a simulation, a period independent of the period used to develop the strategy, which is used to test the strategy.

I

implied volatility   The volatility of an asset implied by the price at which an option on that asset trades. Since the value of an option depends on the price of the underlying asset, the strike price, the volatility of the underlying asset, the riskless rate of interest, and the time remaining to expiration, and since all of these values except volatility are known, volatility can be inferred from the price at which the option trades.

inefficient   The notion that abnormal returns can be achieved from knowledge of past prices, fundamental analysis, or inside information. A revisionist view has emerged which holds that an inefficiency exists only when an arbitrage condition is violated.

initial margin   Funds that must be deposited with a broker (as a form of insurance) to commence a futures transaction.

L

liability-mimicking asset   An asset whose price changes in concert with changes in the value of a pool of liabilities. In the context of assets and liabilities, a liability-mimicking asset is a riskless asset in that it hedges the liabilities.

linear investment rule   A rule used for asset allocation in which the asset mix is determined by multiplying the price-induced change in the percentage allocation to an asset by some factor and adding this value to the asset's previous percentage allocation.

M

market impact   The increase in price from the prior trade that is induced by a buy order or the decrease in price from the prior trade that is induced by a sell order. Market impact costs typically account for the preponderance of transaction costs.

mean reversion   The notion that asset values revert to an average value or to an equilibrium value. Thus, if an asset's price is above its equilibrium value, the presumption of mean reversion is that the asset's price will eventually decline to its equilibrium value, while if its price is below its equilibrium value, the presumption is that the asset's price will eventually rise to its equilibrium value.

mean-variance   An analytical framework in which assets are evaluated according to the mean or expected return and the variance or standard deviation of returns.

multiple   In a constant proportion portfolio insurance strategy, a number greater than one that is used to multiply the difference between the portfolio value and the floor value (cushion) in order to determine the amount to allocate to the risky asset.

N

natural hedge   In the context of assets and liabilities, the extent to which changes in the values of the assets and liabilities are caused by exposure to common factors and thus are mutually offsetting.

net cost of carry   In valuing a financial futures contract, the interest cost associated with purchasing the underlying asset on margin less the income associated with the underlying asset.

net expected return   In the context of assets and liabilities, the expected return of a hypothetical portfolio consisting of a long position in the assets and a short position in the liabilities. In the context of a pension fund, the expected return of the pension fund surplus.

net risk In the context of assets and liabilities, the volatility of a hypothetical portfolio consisting of a long position in the assets and a short position in the liabilities. In the context of a pension fund, the volatility of the pension fund surplus.

net worth In the context of assets and liabilities, the present value of the assets less the present value of the liabilities. In the context of a pension fund, the pension fund surplus.

nonparametric In the context of performance measurement, measures of forecasting ability that do not depend on the ability to predict the magnitude of a return, but rather on the ability to predict the direction of a return.

normal distribution A distribution of outcomes that takes the form of a bell-shaped curve. The normal distribution can be summarized by two statistics, the mean and the variance or standard deviation. Approximately 68 percent of the normal distribution's observations fall within a range defined by the mean minus one standard deviation and the mean plus one standard deviation, whereas 95 percent of the observations are within two standard deviations of the mean.

O

optimal An optimal strategy is one that yields the highest level of expected utility given one's constraints. In strategic asset allocation, the optimal asset mix is defined as that point along the efficient frontier that is tangent to one's utility curve.

original cost protection A constant proportion portfolio insurance strategy in which the floor value is indexed to the starting value of the portfolio.

P

payoff diagram A two-dimensional diagram in which the horizontal axis represents the terminal value of a risky asset and the vertical axis represents the terminal value of alternative strategies involving allocation between a risky asset and a riskless asset or alternative option strategies.

payoff function Within the context of a payoff diagram, a line that relates the terminal value of a particular asset allocation strategy between a risky and a riskless asset or a particular option strategy to the terminal value of the risky asset.

pension fund surplus The present value of pension assets less the present value of pension liabilities.

period specific The notion that a particular result depends on the particular period in which it occurred and that the result is not necessarily characteristic of other past periods or of the future.

portfolio insurance   A dynamic hedging strategy designed to prevent a portfolio from penetrating a prespecified value. It is implemented by shifting assets to a risky component as the portfolio rises in value and to a riskless asset as the portfolio falls in value. The precise amounts to shift are determined by the arbitrage arguments that underlie option valuation. Under perfect market conditions, portfolio insurance produces the same outcome as a protective put option strategy.

portfolio theory   A theory for constructing portfolios that assumes investors choose assets according to their expected return and risk. It relies on the notion that the risk of a portfolio is less than the average risk of its component assets because, to the extent the assets do not move in concert with each other, their risk is diversified away.

program trading   The practice of trading a large package of stocks. The broker may act as agent, in which case he does not assume any principal risk, or he may act as a principal by guaranteeing the prices at which the trades are executed. Program trading is used to effect allocation decisions and to arbitrage misvaluation in the prices of futures contracts on indexes.

protective put option strategy   A strategy whereby a put option is combined with investment in the underlying asset to ensure a minimum return on the combined investment. This strategy produces the same result as a portfolio insurance strategy under perfect market conditions.

put option   A contract that gives the owner the right but not the obligation to sell an asset at a prespecified strike price for a prespecified period of time.

R

random walk   The notion that asset prices change unpredictably just as the next step of a drunk cannot be anticipated.

replacement cost protection   A constant proportion portfolio insurance strategy in which the floor value is continuously indexed to the highest value that the portfolio has reached thus far.

return   The income generated by an asset plus or minus its change in price, all divided by the starting price of the asset.

risk   The uncertainty of an asset's return as described by the variability around the mean return and as measured by the standard deviation of returns.

run   In a time series, a run equals an uninterrupted sequence of positive or negative values or an uninterrupted sequence of values above or below the mean.

S

serial correlation   The association between the prior period's observation and the subsequent period's observation. Positive serial correlation indicates the presence of trends, while negative serial correlation indicates the presence of reversals.

skewness   A situation in which the upper tail of a distribution (values in excess of the median) is more extensive than that of the lower tail (positive skewness) or vice versa (negative skewness).

specific risk   That part of an asset's risk which is unique to the asset and thus can be diversified away by combining the asset in a large portfolio.

standard deviation   A measure of variability that is equal to the square root of the variance and measured in the same units as the variable of interest.

strategic asset allocation   An asset allocation strategy usually based on the principles of portfolio theory. Strategic asset allocation attempts to determine a long-term asset mix for a fund based on the long-term expected return and risk of various asset classes and given an investor's risk preference. Typically, it is not sensitive to the fact that an asset class may be temporarily undervalued or overvalued.

strike price   The prespecified price at which an option may be exercised. In a portfolio insurance strategy, the strike price is analogous to the floor value of the insurance strategy.

systematic risk   That component of an asset's risk which is caused by exposure to sources of risk that are common to many assets, such as sensitivity to interest rates or energy prices. Systematic risk cannot be diversified away, although it can be eliminated through hedging.

T

tactical asset allocation   A valuation-based asset allocation strategy usually based on the presumption of mean reversion. Tactical asset allocation attempts to add value to a fund by shifting away from an asset that appears overvalued and toward an asset that appears undervalued according to some notion of equilibrium or fair value.

time dependence   The notion that a strategy's asset mix or hedge ratio depends on the amount of time remaining in the investment horizon.

t-statistic   In the context of performance measurement, a measure of a result's significance, or more generally, the parameter estimate expressed as a fraction of the standard error.

U

upside capture   In a portfolio insurance strategy, the fraction of the risky asset's terminal value (not return) that is captured by the overall strategy. *Ex ante*, upside capture equals the starting value of the portfolio minus the price of a shadow put option, all divided by the starting value of the portfolio.

utility   A measure of worth for an investor that is conditioned upon his willingness to incur risk in order to increase expected return.

utility curve   In dimensions of expected return and risk, a line that relates an investor's willingness to incur risk in order to increase expected return. A utility curve can also be thought of as a line that connects combinations of expected return and risk between which an investor is indifferent. If expected return is represented by the vertical axis and standard deviation is represented by the horizontal axis, utility curves are convex, indicating that at low levels of expected return an investor is more willing to incur incremental risk in order to increase expected return than he is at higher levels of expected return.

V

variance   A measure of dispersion of a variable computed as the average squared deviation of that variable from its mean value.

variance ratio   The variance estimated from multiple-period intervals divided by the variance estimated from single-period intervals, normalized by dividing this ratio by the number of periods in the interval used to estimate the variance in the numerator. If the observations from which the variance ratio is computed are random, the variance ratio should be close to 1. A variance ratio greater than 1 indicates positive serial correlation, while a variance ratio less than 1 indicates negative serial correlation.

variation margin   In a futures transaction, funds that must be deposited with a broker on a daily basis to cover variation in the price of the underlying asset.

INDEX